Healer of Angels

Martin and Susan Tyner

An Amethyst Moon Book

AMETHYST MOON
PUBLISHING

"In the end, we will conserve only what we love.

We will love only what we understand.

We will understand only what we are taught."

Baba Dioum

"If I can get a child this close to a live eagle,

that child will never hurt an eagle."

Martin Tyner

Healer of Angels

Martin and Susan Tyner

Healer of Angels

Martin and Susan Tyner
P. O. Box 3032
Cedar City, UT 84721-3032
swf@netutah.com
www.gowildlife.org

An Amethyst Moon Book
Published by AMETHYST MOON PUBLISHING
P. O. Box 87885
Tucson, AZ 85754
www.onechoicecanchangealife.com

First Edition 2009

ISBN 978-1-935354-12-3 (13 digit)
1-935354-12-4 (10 digit)

Dedication

We would like to dedicate this book to our children, grandchildren and great grandchildren, and to everyone who has ever cared for a sick, injured, or orphaned creature. THANK YOU!

Acknowledgments

A special THANK YOU to all of our friends who have encouraged us every step of the way. Noella Ballenger, a gifted photographer and dear friend, I like to call her my head cheerleader. Ann and Stan Westfall, without their love and generosity many of the photographs in this book would not be possible. Sue Arnold and Joanne Browne for their help, patience and encouragement. There are so many friends who have helped, unfortunately there is no way to name them all. Dear friends, you will always have my deepest appreciation for everything that you have done.

It's been said many times, "Behind every great man, is a good woman." In my case, not only behind a good man, but right beside me, is a great woman, my wife, Susan. Susan has not only been the love of my life, she is my best friend, my partner, my confidante. When I could not find the strength to go on, my sweet Susan has always been willing to take the lead. All that I am and all that I have would not be possible without the love and support of this amazing young lady.

--*Martin Tyner*

Contents

Part One: The Hunt *by Susan Tyner*

In a steady cold wind on a late January afternoon, snow crunched underfoot as the old falconer climbed higher up the ridge of an ancient lava flow. He came here often to find his inner strength and peace. His green eyes misted over as he faced into the wind, its chill as refreshing to his soul as its bitter harshness was biting to his face.

As he reached the top he scanned the distances to the north and south along the ridge. The wind continued to blow from the southwest. It was a clear day, but he knew the clouds of another winter storm would be coming soon. The sun shining in the sky gave little warmth that day, but there was warmth deep inside him that spread as he watched his golden eagle soaring effortlessly a few hundred yards away.

His light brown hair was in need of a trim. He pulled out a warm hat from his coat pocket and covered his head and ears to keep out the cold. Deep lines were etched in his face from years of being out in the drying sun and wind. Yet, you also saw the little laugh lines around his eyes.

He was wearing blue jeans and a flannel shirt. His boots were worn but comfortable. He had on a warm brown coat and a green hunting vest. A small whistle hung from a leather lace around his neck. On his left hand he wore a heavy, leather glove that extended to his elbow.

A smile tipped the corners of his mouth as he watched his eagle soar along the ridge. Suddenly the eagle retracted its wings diving vertically at well over a hundred miles an hour. It crashed through the sage as a jackrabbit bolted from the brush and ran a short distance up the hillside and into the safety of the rocks, out of danger of the eagle's large, crushing talons. The eagle landed on a large rock near where the rabbit had disappeared, clearly disappointed.

Spreading his wings once again the eagle lifted from the rocks to soar along the ridge. As he gained altitude he turned back toward the old man with an outstretched arm. As the eagle approached he flared his wings and tail, then gently landed on the glove. The eagle reached down and retrieved a small portion of meat hidden between the fingers of the glove, which he swallowed quickly.

With the tidbit gone, the eagle launched from the glove and returned to the sky. As he watched his eagle soar effortlessly, the old falconer took a moment to reflect back on his life and the experiences that had brought him to this place and time.

Part Two: Early Childhood

George the Pigeon

As a young child, barely a toddler, I reached into the cage of the family parakeet trying to pet the brightly-colored, green bird. As my fingers drew close, the small bird, attempting to defend itself, bit my finger.

I screamed loudly. As I pulled my hand back, both the cage and I tumbled to the ground. This trauma not only frightened both the small bird and me, but it started me on a series of events that would one day guide my destiny.

After that one incident, I became terrified of birds. At two or maybe three years of age, whenever I saw a robin or any small bird fly overhead I would scream and run for the house. Birds were flighty, scary, and they could bite!

One day my grandmother heard a loud scream coming from the backyard. As she opened the door I came running into her arms trembling with fear. She spent the next few minutes trying to calm me down, and then asked, "What's wrong?"

I pointed out the window, with tears streaming down my face I was sobbing so hard that I could barely say the word "BIRD." The encounter with the parakeet had affected me far more than anyone could have imagined.

My grandmother, being the wise woman that she was, believed that fear was a limitation and that you should have no limitations on your life. So Grandma went out and bought me a pet pigeon, a common grey barn pigeon. My grandfather and I worked together to build a large pine and chicken wire cage. It was a home for the pigeon. The pigeon's name was George.

For the next few months one of my chores at Grandma's house was to give George food and water, which meant that I had to put my hand in the cage. At first this was difficult. With kind and gentle support from my grandparents I learned to stick my hand in the cage and to fill the dishes with fresh food and water. As the weeks went by this became the highlight of my day. You see, George was my first pet.

By the end of the summer, I could open the cage and George would fly around free. He would allow me to hold him and pet him. He had the most beautiful, soft pigeon coo. One of the things that drew us closest together was when I would let George out of the cage and he would fly around and poop on my older brother. My older brother was twice as big as I was and quite the bully. So George was my defender and my friend.

From that moment on I developed a fascination not only with birds, but with animals in general. My grandmother and I would frequently go to the local library and check out books on animals, and of course birds were always my favorite.

Books and Beginnings

Playa Del Ray Elementary was a small inner city school; not a blade of grass, not a flower, not a tree. The playground areas were asphalt. The school buildings were typical, rectangular box-shaped structures with light pink stucco walls and very few windows. All of the buildings looked the same with the exception of the temporary trailer classrooms brought in to help with overcrowding.

The classrooms were all the same: metal chairs, steel tables with wooden tops. The teachers did their best to give these classrooms a bit of personality with crepe paper and pictures taped to the walls. The school was surrounded by low income housing and apartment buildings.

This is where I first realized that I was different; I had a problem. I was generally a happy child, a little smaller than most of the other children, and a little shy of my surroundings. I was now seven years old and had just entered the second grade.

I don't remember the teacher's name; I'll just call her, "Mrs. Wright." She was a large woman, heavy set, with salt and pepper hair. She usually wore a dress with a flower pattern. Your first impression would be that of a kind, middle-aged woman who had been teaching elementary school for many, many years.

The first few days of class, studies and orientation seemed to go well, but things would soon become very difficult. Each of the students in class was handed a book, a second grade reader. I'm sure you remember the type. You know, *"Run Spot Run,"* with lots of pictures and a few words to start the children on their path to reading.

Mrs. Wright would call all of her students to form a circle in the center of classroom. She would ask each of us to open the book to a specific page and each student would be asked to read a sentence. If you were unable to read the sentence she would read it to you and then request that you read it back to her and then it was the next child's turn.

As the days and weeks passed it became very obvious which of the children could read and which of the children could not. Every day as reading time approached, I became more and more uncomfortable. When the teacher would call my name, immediately some of the children would begin to snicker. Any mistakes that I made were immediately corrected with a strong and impatient voice.

By the end of the first semester there were a few of us that were separated out from the rest of the children. We each sat in a corner and listened to the other children read. Occasionally one of us would be called upon to read a paragraph.

I would stutter and stumble over words. Immediately Mrs. Wright's voice would roar, "That's wrong! When are you going to learn?"

I felt embarrassed, stupid and ashamed as the other children laughed.

After the first semester, during a parent teacher conference, I remember listening to Mrs. Wright explain to my mother, "I have done all that I can and most likely Martin will never learn to read, but as long as there is a need for ditch diggers Martin will probably be fine."

Toward the end of second grade all of the children were required to take a government sponsored IQ test. Mrs. Wright explained that this would determine our future and the results of this test would affect us for the rest of our lives. Of course you could only imagine how poorly I did on the test.

At the end of the school year my test results were made known to my mother. It was obvious to her that I had limitations and probably would not have the kind of successful life that my brother and sister could and would have.

Grandma's House

After the summer I entered the third grade. My teacher was made aware of my disability, so very little was expected of me. At the end of the semester my grandmother was over for a visit, and lying on the kitchen counter was my report card.

When she saw the report card, which was mostly D's and F's, she called me into the house. With a look that only a staunch, Iowa farm woman could give, my grandmother asked me, "What's this?"

You see, my grandmother was a retired school teacher.

I replied, "That's my report card."

In a strong voice she said "No, what are these grades?"

I replied, "My mom and my teacher told me that I'm not smart and that I will never be able to be like my brother and sister, so this is the best I can do."

The look in my grandmother's eyes I will never forget: a mixture of anger, frustration and determination. She grabbed me by the scruff, hauled me to the kitchen table, sat me down, looked me square in the eyes and said, "I know you, and I know that you are as smart as your brother and sister, maybe even more so. From now on, every day after school you are coming to my house."

So every day after school, off to Grandma's house I went. At first it felt like a punishment, sitting at the kitchen table when all the other children were out playing. We spent hours, and hours, and hours with flash cards; hours of reading, writing, and math.

I began to enjoy all of this personal attention with my grandmother. After my studies, Grandma and I would walk to the grocery store and then down the block to the library where I could pick out any book I wanted.

I chose mostly books on animals, dinosaurs and airplanes, whatever caught my interest. It really didn't matter. What did matter was the time my grandmother spent with me sitting at the kitchen table reading books and then afterwards baking a batch of our favorite oatmeal chocolate chip cookies. These are some of my fondest childhood memories.

Grandma's Old Fashioned Oatmeal Chocolate Chip Cookies

Throughout my life when things got hard and my world was spinning out of control, and it felt that there was nothing I could do to stop it, I would bake a batch of my grandma's oatmeal chocolate chip cookies. There was something amazing about Grandma's cookies and I would like to share her recipe with you.

First, gather family, friends or loved ones. If family, friends or loved ones are not available, **perfect** strangers work just fine.

You may ask, "Where can I find **perfect** strangers?"

Perfect strangers can be found at your local church, mosque, synagogue, or temple. **Perfect** strangers can be found in hospitals, homeless shelters, retirement homes, scout troops, libraries, and schools. After you have gathered up the appropriate number of friends, family, loved ones, or **perfect** strangers, it is now time to mix the cookie dough.

In a large mixing bowl add:

½ cup Crisco
1 cup sugar
2 beaten eggs
½ cup milk

1 teaspoon vanilla

Mix well.

In a second bowl mix:

2 cups oatmeal
2 cups flour
1 small teaspoon baking soda
¼ teaspoon salt

Slowly add the dry ingredients to the wet ingredients. Mix with an old fashioned wooden spoon until your arm is tired, and then pass it off to someone else.

When thoroughly mixed, stir in:

½ cup chopped walnuts
¾ cup chocolate bits

Preheat oven to 350 degrees.

Place heaping teaspoon-sized balls of dough on a cookie sheet and bake for 8 to 10 minutes.

As the cookies bake, break out your favorite board game or card game and sit around the kitchen table telling stories and discussing your hopes and dreams. Pass around the warm freshly baked cookies until everyone has had their fill.

Grandma's old fashioned oatmeal chocolate chip cookies cannot heal the sick, raise the dead, or pay my bills, but with a little help from my friends, Grandma's cookies can give me the strength to face life's problems and hardships. As I said, "Grandma's cookies are amazing."

Dyslexia, Overcoming Hurdles

My life soon took a dramatic turn. We moved from Culver City, California, to Simi Valley, a small agriculture community about forty-five miles north of Los Angeles.

If there was ever such a place as heaven on earth, this was it! Orange groves, walnut groves and rolling foothills surrounding a small valley. This was a place of freedom for a reasonably shy child who did not make friends easily. To be able to wander the fields and foothills and to watch hawks, eagles and condors fly.

These wild places became my sanctuary. Unfortunately, they didn't help my school work. Reading and writing was still a significant problem, and now I was not able to go to Grandma's house everyday after school.

I spent most of my weekends and my summers with my grandparents. As hard as we worked, it was obvious to me and to everyone else that I was different.

For some reason I was quite the inventor. I could look at a mechanical problem and fix it. I seemed to have a deeper understanding of the wild creatures around me. Eventually, with the help of my grandparents I came to the conclusion that I wasn't dumb, just different.

All through my school years I struggled to understand why I was different. It certainly wasn't for a lack of trying and it wasn't for a lack of help.

One day when I was in my mid-twenties, I was watching a news story on television about a learning disability called "dyslexia." It was like someone flipped a switch! I was shocked! Now it all began to make sense. I found out that my brain processed information differently. Once I understood, I knew I could make the necessary adjustments. I found myself achieving my life's goals and achieving far more than anyone, including myself, could have ever believed.

Raining Frogs

After we moved to Simi Valley I entered the fourth grade at Vista Elementary School. It was a new school and a new teacher. I desperately wanted to make a good impression. Mrs. Lee was in the process of creating a terrarium for the class and asked if any of the students knew where they could find small lizards or frogs to place in the terrarium. Immediately my hand went up, "Mrs. Lee, I know where there are a bunch of frogs!"

Mrs. Lee said, "Can you bring some frogs to school tomorrow morning?" and I answered, "You bet!"

I was very excited. I could barely wait for the school day to end. At three o'clock the bell rang and I bolted out of my chair, headed for my bicycle and then racing for home.

When I arrived home I searched the garage to find some kind of container that would hold a whole bunch of frogs. You see, I may not have been a good reader, but I was a great frog catcher!

I found a large half-gallon size jar in the back of the pantry with a twist on metal top. I punched a few holes in the metal top with a screwdriver and off I went to a small stream that bubbled from a spring at the base of the foothills about two miles from my home.

This was one of my secret places. The stream ran underneath a giant white oak tree and the stream bank was lined with cattails and reeds. If you sat quietly up in the oak tree you could watch raccoons fishing for crayfish in the stream and the occasional deer or coyote coming down to the stream for a drink. But on that day, more important than the deer or the coyotes were the frogs. There were thousands of tiny, bright, lime green tree frogs everywhere.

I spent the next couple of hours catching frogs along the stream till the bottle was filled with what seemed like hundreds of frogs. There were probably only fifty or so, but it seemed like hundreds.

I headed for home with my bottle of frogs. I just knew that Mrs. Lee would be very impressed with my giant bottle of frogs. I woke up early the next morning. I had been almost too excited to sleep. When it was finally time to leave home, I hopped on my bicycle with my bottle of frogs and headed for school.

When I arrived at school the other children were excited to see the frogs. As I entered Mrs. Lee's classroom she was very busy at her desk. Just as the school bell rang I said, "Mrs. Lee, I've got a bottle of frogs for your terrarium!"

Without looking up Mrs. Lee said, "Just put them in the terrarium and take your seat."

I walked over to the terrarium, which was a twenty-gallon glass aquarium with a little bit of water, bark and plants for the animals to hide in. I noticed that the terrarium did not have a cover. By that time all of the other children were coming through the classroom door, and I asked Mrs. Lee, "Where's the cover for the terrarium?"

Again Mrs. Lee said, "Just put the frogs in the terrarium and take your seat."

So I poured the frogs into the terrarium and quickly took my seat.

Mrs. Lee stood up from her desk and began to call roll, "Jeff Allen," and the student said, "Here."

"Sherry Barker."

"Here."

I looked over toward the terrarium. Oh, my gosh...not only were the frogs coming out of the terrarium, but they were climbing the walls! I raised my hand and said, "Mrs. Lee, Mrs. Lee, the frogs!" But Mrs. Lee said, "Martin, put your hand down, we'll talk about your frogs later."

So I sat quietly as Mrs. Lee continued to call roll and read the morning announcements to the class. By now the frogs were all over the walls and crawling across the ceiling.

All of a sudden one of the frogs fell from the ceiling and landed on Cindy Everett's desk. She screamed and jumped from her desk as frogs started to rain down on the students below. Frogs landed in children's hair and in their laps. By now there were frogs everywhere, and children were screaming. Mrs. Lee was desperate to get control of the class and get the students out of the classroom. When all of the students were assembled outside of the classroom Mrs. Lee said, "Martin, what have you done?"

I tried to explain that I had asked about a lid for the terrarium, but Mrs. Lee wasn't going to hear any of it. She demanded that I go back into the classroom and remove every frog from her class.

While the rest of the students had a day-long recess playing kickball and having fun, I spent the day in Mrs. Lee's class trying to catch every frog. The frogs were not only on the walls and ceiling, they were in the bookshelves, under the desks, in the light fixtures — they were everywhere! I caught as many frogs as I could find and placed them back in the bottle.

For the rest of the school year there would be the occasional dried up, dead frog behind a book, under a shelf, or in the back of a cupboard. Mrs. Lee would yell at me to go get the frog and get it out of her class. I certainly made an impression on Mrs. Lee, but it just wasn't a good one.

Grandpa's Pocket Watch

The greatest man I've ever known was my grandpa. To the world he was a short, slender, bald-headed, quiet gentleman that drove a laundry truck. He always wore brown slacks, a plaid shirt and a light brown cap. Every evening around five o'clock Grandpa would arrive home, much to the delight of my brother, sister and I.

We would kneel on the old green couch in front of the living room window, watching for Grandpa to pull into the driveway in his large, white step van with the name BEACON written across the side.

As he pulled into the driveway, we would run out the front door of the house and he would slide open the door of the truck. After piling into the van and giving Grandpa big hugs, we'd hold on tight as Grandpa drove the van forward about fifty feet to its parking space in front of the garage. Then we would all jump from the van, climb the steps of the back porch, and run into the house where Grandma was putting the final touches on dinner.

After Grandpa came home it was time to get cleaned up for dinner. We washed all the dirt and mud off our hands and faces, and took our places around the kitchen table. Meals were simple: casseroles, spaghetti, macaroni and cheese, with fresh vegetables from the garden and homemade bread. When dinner was over, and if I'd completed all of my studies and homework, Grandpa and I would go out to the garage and work on a project. Whether it was fixing Grandma's old toaster or working on our soapbox derby car made out of wooden crates, two by fours and wagon wheels, there were always projects that Grandpa and I were working on.

Grandma may have been a school teacher, but the lessons I learned from Grandpa were just as important. Grandpa taught me how to shoot marbles, spin a wooden top, how to win at pick-up sticks, how to bait a hook, catch a fish, and most of all, how to be a good father.

During our activities together, Grandpa used to impart small bits of wisdom. Grandpa used to say, "There is no shame in being a gopher, as long as you are a darn good gopher." (A gopher is someone who is a laborer that is told to go for this and go for that.)

Every morning when my grandpa would leave for work he would say, "Martin, do good today." Grandpa believed in a very simple philosophy; that a person should get up every morning and do good. Grandpa taught me the difference between doing good and doing well.

Doing good means that you do well for others and doing well means that you do good for yourself. There is nothing wrong with doing well, but Grandpa always believed in doing good.

One Saturday afternoon when I was nine years old, Grandpa called me into the living room where he reached out his arms and invited me to join him in his big, brown recliner chair. Grandpa's chair was really cool. Not only was it big and comfortable, but you could push back and the chair would recline and the footrest would come up. It was a great place to take a nap. The chair had a small electrical switch on the right side and when you flipped the switch the whole chair would vibrate.

This time when Grandpa invited me to jump up into his lap he seemed almost sad and very serious. Grandpa said he needed to talk to me, and with a concerned look on his face he reached into the left pocket of his brown trousers and pulled out a gold pocket watch.

He said, "This watch has been in the family for over a hundred years and the watch has always been passed down from father to son. Before the son can receive the watch he must make a promise and keep the promise. The promise is that the son will not drink, smoke, do drugs, or get thrown in jail until after they've reached the age of twenty-one."

Grandpa continued, "My three sons, your uncles, were unable to keep the promise. They all drank or smoked before the age of twenty-one, so I still have the watch. Martin, would you make this promise to not drink, smoke, do drugs, or get thrown in jail until after you are twenty-one, so that I may pass on the watch to you?"

I've never seen Grandpa like this. A single tear formed at the edge of his right eye as I made the promise, "Grandpa, I promise I will not drink, smoke, do drugs, or get thrown in jail until after I am twenty-one."

Grandpa hugged me tight, and I could feel the burden and the sadness lift from Grandpa's heart. Grandpa said, "We need some of Grandma's chocolate chip cookies and milk." So as I jumped down off of Grandpa's lap, we headed for the kitchen and the cookie jar.

At that time, I did not understand the impact that promise would have on my life. Going through high school in the late sixties and early seventies, drugs and alcohol were present at every party and at every teenage event. Whenever a friend would offer me a drink, a smoke or a pill and try to convince me that getting high was really cool, I would remember my promise and Grandpa's face and that single tear.

Grandpa passed away when I was nineteen and no one in the family remembered the promise, so I never got the watch. People often say, "How sad, you never got the watch." The pocket watch was never the point. The true gift from my grandfather was the promise.

Part Three: Path to Falconry

My First Owl

I was twelve years old and most of the people in the neighborhood knew that I had a fondness for birds. I was always picking up orphaned sparrows and robins and trying to raise them, frequently without success.

One day a neighbor from down the block showed up at our front door with a large cardboard box and asked if I still liked birds.

"Of course I still like birds," I replied.

He handed me the cardboard box and said, "Here is a baby bird that has fallen from its nest, see what you can do with it."

As the neighbor left I picked up the box, turned, walked into the house and placed the box on the living room floor. As I started to open the box I heard the most horrifying sound. This was no bird. If you could image the sound of a hissing snake, but hundreds of times louder. The box started to bang and bump, so I held the lid closed for a few moments, afraid that whatever was in the box would escape. Who knows, it was probably poisonous.

After whatever it was that was in the box quieted down, I decided to open the box more slowly and see if I could get a glimpse of whatever it was. As I slowly peeled the top open, I could see lots of soft, white fluffy – something? It looked almost like a giant cotton ball. As I slid the top of the box further back, the horrible sound started again. Hissing, growling, whatever you want to call it. Whatever it was, it had to be possessed by the devil!

I paused for a moment and the sound quieted down, so I continued to remove the top and in the large cardboard box was the ugliest animal I've ever seen. The head and body were pure white, soft and fluffy, with the ugliest prehistoric face that you could imagine. It had a large hooked beak and pure black eyes that stared back at me. This wasn't the face of a bird. It looked like the face had been smashed inward. Below that soft, white, fluffy body was a huge

23

set of claws. This animal stood in the box, rocking back and forth, twisting its head from side to side and growling violently at me. It may have been a bird, but this was a monster bird, not the typical pigeons and sparrows that I was used to.

I put the lid back on the box and went to my book shelf and picked up a copy of *Birds of America*. As I hunted through the book looking at all the pictures, I decided that it must be some kind of an owl, probably a barn owl.

I picked up the box and took it into my bedroom and placed it on my bed. I then headed outside, jumped on my bicycle and rode to the local library to find all of the information I could on owls.

The first thing I discovered was that owls have razor sharp claws, so I was going to have to use my father's leather work gloves to handle this animal. The next thing I found out was that they eat small rodents: mice, kangaroo rats, gophers. Living next to the fields, we seemed to have an endless supply of those little critters, so I started setting out mouse traps to catch food for the baby owl.

Martin Tyner

The mouse traps very quickly started to pay off and our family pet, a cat named Mazda, who was a great mouser in her own right, was helping in the effort. I was Mazda's favorite person and she would frequently bring me gifts. Every evening when I would get ready for bed, I would have to be very careful because Mazda liked to hide live mice under my pillow. That was her way of saying that she loved me.

With a couple of dead mice in hand, I put on my father's work gloves and slowly opened the top of the box. The owl immediately started to rock back and forth, twisting his head from side to side and growling violently. By now my parents were home and hearing the awful sound coming from my bedroom they opened the door and asked, "What have you got now?"

I told them, "A neighbor down the street found this baby owl that had fallen from its nest and brought it here so that I could care for it."

Needless to say, my parents were pretty unhappy. My mother wanted it out of the house, now! So I took the owl out to the backyard and placed it in an old pigeon coop that I had in a back corner of the yard. I really didn't think that was fair. Yes, the owl was loud and scary, but it was only a baby and it needed to be cared for.

With a glove on my hand, I took one of the mice and I held my hand down in the box as the owl growled and rocked its head. After a couple of minutes he grabbed my hand with his right foot and began to feed on the mouse. After the first mouse was gone, I handed him the second and that one was devoured just as quickly.

It became obvious I was going to have a full time job just trying to keep this owl fed. I went out several times a day checking the mouse traps and for the first time, I really appreciated Mazda's live mouse presents under my pillow.

When some of the neighbors found out that I had an owl that needed to be fed, they would bring me mice and gophers that they had killed in their yards. I don't think my mother appreciated the dead mice and gophers on the bottom shelf of the refrigerator.

I was so excited. I had read books on falconry, the art of training birds of prey to be your hunting companion. I knew that this barn owl would be the greatest hunter in the world.

He grew very quickly. In a matter of weeks all that white fluffy down was replaced by beautiful, golden feathers across his back

25

and wings, and pure white feathers on the underside of his wings and body. He was large and beautiful and he loved to eat mice. I would bring him in the house and let him fly (when my parents weren't home) and he would land on my arm for food.

Game Warden Bob

One day I went grocery shopping with my mother. I overheard a gentleman in a green and brown uniform talking about hunting and fishing. It was Game Warden Bob! I knew Game Warden Bob. He had come to my school!

I walked up to him and said, "Hi Game Warden Bob, you came to my school, and I like hunting and fishing. I have a barn owl and he is going to be the best hunting bird ever!"

The game warden looked down at me and said, "Do you have an owl?"

I proudly said, "Yes I do."

The game warden asked, "Son, where do you live?"

I said, "Just a few blocks from here," and I gave him my address.

The next evening Game Warden Bob was knocking at my front door. He said, "You are the young man that has the owl."

I said, "Yes, I am."

Then he asked, "Are your parents home?"

I called to my mother and said, "Mom, Game Warden Bob wants to talk to you."

As my mother approached the front door the game warden began to explain that I could not have an owl for a pet and that he would need to confiscate it.

I was crushed. My owl, my hunter, my companion, my friend, was being taken away. I had gone to so much work finding food for him and giving him a good home, and now Game Warden Bob was stealing him from me. I went to my room and cried for hours. It wasn't fair, but my owl was gone.

A couple of weeks went by and life was back to normal, wandering out through the fields catching lizards and snakes, watching the hawks and vultures soar overhead, and reading every book on birds of prey and falconry that I could find.

One evening there was a knock on the door. It was Game Warden Bob. Boy was I mad! How dare he come back here after stealing my owl?

He asked, "Are your parents home?

I said, "Yes." I called my mother to the front door and told her, "Mom, the game warden wants to talk to you."

He asked my mother if she would mind him giving me a bird, something that was a little more appropriate for falconry. I couldn't believe it. I asked him, "Are you going to give me back my owl?"

He said, "No, but I've got another orphaned animal that would be better suited for falconry." He opened up a large cardboard box that was sitting on the ground next to him and there was a giant ball of light grey fluff, with a large, hooked beak, brown eyes, giant sharp claws, but no sound. It just sat in the box quietly. It was a baby red tailed hawk.

I looked at my Mom and said, "Please, please, please!"

As she shook her head no she said, "It better never come in the house and I don't ever want to see dead gophers or mice in the kitchen sink again."

I promised her that she would never know that it was there if she would just let me have it.

She reluctantly said, "OK."

I thanked Game Warden Bob, picked up the large cardboard box and started to head into the house as my mother said sternly, "Martin!"

I said, "Oh, yeah, I'm sorry," so I opened the garage door and walked around to the back of the yard where the pigeon loft sat empty and waiting.

It wasn't long before Game Warden Bob was regularly bringing me sick, injured and orphaned critters.

Meeting Hubert

In the spring of 1972 I jumped into my 1956 Volkswagen Bug. Oh my gosh, it was the ugliest car you've ever seen. It was brown on the outside, pumpkin orange on the inside. The fenders and bumpers were held on with baling wire and with its little forty-six horse motor, it could barely get out of its own way.

The speed limit back then was fifty-five miles an hour, which was just fine because the only time the Volkswagen Bug could make it to fifty-five miles an hour was when it was going downhill. It was my first car and to me it was beautiful, when it wasn't breaking down.

I was driving on a small winding road behind Lake Sherwood looking for Cooper's hawks when I heard an amazing sound, something right out of a Tarzan movie! I stopped the old Volkswagen Bug and turned off the motor to hear if the sound was truly what I thought it was, or maybe it was just the old car breaking down again.

There it was again, it sounded like an elephant. The trumpeting sound echoed through the canyon. Off to my left I noticed a small gravel driveway that dropped deep into the canyon through the oak trees. I decided to explore and find out where the sound was coming from.

About two hundred yards down the small gravel road at the bottom of the canyon there was an older gentleman wearing a khaki shirt, khaki shorts and sandals. He was walking an elephant ... a huge, massive, grey African elephant.

About fifty yards behind the elephant there was a series of large cages. One held an African lion and another, a black bear. I wasn't sure what to do. I was tremendously curious and I was also a little scared. Then I noticed perches in the shade under a giant white oak tree. Sitting on the perches were some of the most beautiful birds of prey that I had ever seen. An eagle, hawks, falcons and owls, most of them I could not identify. They were certainly not North American birds of prey.

The eagle was a martial eagle from Africa, a little larger than our North American golden eagle and more brightly colored. There was an eagle-owl, similar in color to our great horned owl, but it had to be at least three times larger, and there were exotic hawks and falcons from the far corners of the world.

My desire to see these animals up close overcame my fear. So I continued walking down the gravel road calling out in my loudest voice, "Hello."

The older gentleman yelled back, "Stay where you are. Don't come any closer."

I froze in my tracks. For the next few minutes I stood motionless, watching him as he worked his elephant. The elephant would pick up its feet, lean back as if it was sitting on its behind, raise its trunk and trumpet loudly. She would lean forward bending the front legs at the knees as if to bow to her trainer. She would turn circles to the right and circles to the left following her trainer's every command.

When the training session was over, the trainer walked the elephant to a shady area next to a large watering trough. The elephant stood perfectly still. She raised her left front foot as the trainer wrapped a chain around her leg, the elephant then placed her foot back on the ground and then she began splashing and playing with the water.

The elephant trainer turned his attention back to me and yelled, "This is private property, you are not allowed to be here."

I yelled back, "My name is Martin, and I'm a falconer. May I come look at your birds?"

He yelled back very precise instructions on the direction that I must go to approach the area where the birds were perched and not to disturb the other animals in the compound. I followed his instructions to the letter and he met me just before I reached the area where the birds were perched.

Quite by accident I had stumbled across the wildlife compound of Hubert Wells, the owner of Animal Actors of Hollywood. I walked up and introduced myself, "Hi, my name is Martin Tyner and I am a falconer."

Mr. Hubert Wells leaned his head slightly to one side and with a thick Hungarian accent asked me, "Why are you here?"

I explained that I was driving up the canyon looking for Cooper's hawks when I had heard his elephant trumpet. My curiosity had gotten the better of me and I wanted to see where the sound had come from. I explained again that I was a falconer and I saw his beautiful birds sitting on their perches in the shade. I asked Mr. Wells, "Are you a falconer as well?"

Again, cocking his head slightly to the side and with a somewhat stern and impatient voice he said, "I am a falconer, my father was a falconer, and my grandfather was a falconer. What would you like to know about my birds?"

At that moment I realized that I was standing in the presence of a true multi-generational Hungarian falconer. Maybe, for the first time in my life, I had absolutely nothing to say; so I decided to listen to Mr. Wells and try to absorb anything and everything that he would be willing to teach me.

After a short description of his birds and a quick tour of his animal compound Mr. Wells said that he must get back to work and that I must leave. I asked him if I might come back another day and visit with him again.

With some hesitation he said that I may come back as long as I stay out of his way and don't get close to the animals.

I quickly left the compound, walked back to the road, jumped in the old Volkswagen Bug and headed for home.

Animal Actors

Saturday morning I got up early. I made sure that all of my chores around the house were done as quickly as possible. I did not want to waste a second. I jumped in my car and with a quick prayer, fingers crossed, knock on wood and a little bit of coaxing; I turned the key and the engine started, so off I headed to Animal Actors of Hollywood.

I pulled off the windy mountain road and onto a small dirt patch next to the driveway that led down to the animal compound. I could hear elephants, lions, chimpanzees, hyenas, sea lions, and birds of every description. As I approached the bottom of the canyon I called out to Mr. Wells and he hollered back, "Stay where you are!"

Again I froze, not moving a muscle. Off to my right approximately twenty feet away a large Siberian tiger appeared from behind one of the compounds dragging a chain. My heart almost leapt out of my chest until I realized that on the other end of the chain was Mr. Wells. He quickly moved the tiger through a chain link gate and into a freshly cleaned compound where the tiger jumped on top of a large plywood box, stretched and laid down.

Mr. Wells quietly retreated from the tiger enclosure, locked the gate behind him and walked directly to me. Without explanation he said, "Follow me." We walked through the gate and into the main compound, to a wheelbarrow and a shovel and the largest pile of poop that I had ever seen. He said, "If you are going to be here, you've got chores to do." So I walked over to the pile of elephant dung, filled the wheelbarrow and then pushed the wheelbarrow about three hundred yards to the far end of the property where there was a giant mulch pit. This process was repeated about a dozen times.

After the elephant dung was removed, I was called to bring the wheelbarrow and the shovel to a large chain-link compound where the Siberian tiger had just been removed. I was instructed to pick up all of the feces, to clean and rake until the facility was spotless.

I was also instructed to pick up a bucket full of water mixed with a disinfectant soap and scrub the concrete pad and the concrete house from top to bottom, and to finish it off by rinsing everything with a hose.

Once the compound was cleaned the tiger was returned, then the lion was moved and I started the process all over again. After the lion, it was the wolves, after the wolves it was the bear. After a day of shoveling poop, scrubbing and disinfecting the compounds I was tired, I smelled really bad and had blisters on my hands. Then with a big smile on his face, Hubert said, "I'll see you tomorrow."

So I hiked up the driveway out of the canyon. With sore muscles I could barely make it to the car. Thank goodness the car started because I just didn't have the energy to push it. I headed for home.

Learning From The Master

The next day I arrived at the compound at eight o'clock in the morning. I hollered out in a loud voice, "Good Morning," and soon Mr. Wells appeared at the gate. He tipped his head slightly to the side and with a puzzled look on his face he said, "You're back?"

I replied, "Yes sir."

Mr. Wells, without explanation said, "Follow me."

As we walked away from the compound toward the far end of his property I noticed a half a dozen post holes had been dug and there was a large amount of pipe and chain-link fencing. With a smile on his face he turned back toward the compound and said, "The post holes are marked, get to work."

I stood there for a moment a bit confused. Not knowing what else to do, I picked up the post-hole digger and got to work.

Around four o'clock in the afternoon, Mr. Wells showed up and said, "See you tomorrow."

I replied, "I have school tomorrow, but I'll see you next Saturday."

Again I walked up out of the canyon to the car, exhausted. For the very first time I was grateful for school. I had never worked so hard in my life.

For the next few months, I rolled out of bed early on Saturday and Sunday mornings and headed for Animal Actors. Each morning Mr. Wells looked surprised when I'd show up. Nevertheless, he always had a long list of chores for me to do. I would finish the chores and go home. By this time I was really beginning to wonder what I had gotten myself into.

Then one Saturday morning when I arrived, Mr. Wells said, "Please call me Hubert." With a smile on his face he said, "I want you to walk the elephant."

For the second time in my life, I didn't know what to say. The elephant's name was Mombasa. She was a beautiful fifteen year old African elephant. Hubert handed me the walking stick, and I spent the morning exercising the elephant, learning the commands, and learning the hand gestures. We walked the elephant over to a large concrete pad where there was a water faucet and a hose. Hubert handed me a bucket of soapy water and a large scrub brush. I gave the command, "Down," and the elephant lowered itself to its knees. Both the elephant and I were about to have our bath for the day.

She seemed to enjoy the attention; she always enjoyed the water. I began scrubbing her left side, then behind her left ear. Suddenly she rolled toward me, onto her left side. I quickly jumped out of the way. Walking around to the right side she laid there as I scrubbed every inch of her body. Then she rolled to her right and I repeated scrubbing the left side of her body. I gave the command to stand. Hubert and I walked around Mombasa as she lifted each of her legs so we could inspect the health of her feet and make sure that her toenails were not overgrown.

Now that bath time was over, all by myself, I walked her back to the large trough where she picked up her left front foot. I placed the chain around her leg, and she started to play in the water. I was already soaked to the bone. To add insult to injury she stuck her trunk in the water trough, sucked up a couple gallons of water and sprayed me in the face. Hubert stood about fifty feet away with a big smile on his face and he said, "See you tomorrow."

Hubert Wells became my mentor and my friend. Over the next several years I took every opportunity to visit Animal Actors. Although there were always chores to be done, the chores became far more interesting. Always under Hubert's careful supervision, I was given the opportunity to care for the beautiful and exotic creatures that he owned. He also helped me to develop my falconry skills.

Whenever I found myself having a problem with one of the animals, (whatever I was doing wasn't working) I would look over to Hubert and he'd have a big smile on his face. This was his way of saying, "When you're done doing it wrong, ask me and I'll teach you how to do it right."

He would never interrupt a training session by saying, "Do it this way." He would allow me to struggle until either I figured it out or asked for help.

Part Four: Working with Wildlife

Vulture Vomit

Turkey vultures to most people are ugly, black birds with bald, red heads and a disgusting habit of feeding on dead, rotting carcasses. In reality they're one of God's most perfectly designed creatures. They feed on dead deer, sheep, and cows, whatever they can find. They help keep the mountains and deserts clean, preventing the spread of disease.

They will often stick their head up inside the abdominal cavity to feed on the guts, getting blood on their heads. If the vulture had feathers on the top of its head like an eagle has, the blood would mat the feathers down, causing infection and the bird would get sick. With the bald head, the blood just dries and flakes off. This helps to keep the vulture clean.

It was a warm spring afternoon when my best friend and I decided that it would be a lot of fun to drive through the coastal foothills of Southern California, out to a vulture's nest that we had found a couple of weeks earlier. We wanted to take pictures of the baby vultures.

We jumped into my buddy's 1955 Chevy pickup truck and headed out for our day's adventure. We parked the truck as close as we could to the vulture's nest, grabbed all of our ropes and climbing gear from the back of the truck and began the hour's walk to the ridge line. The vulture's nest sat on a rocky outcropping at the top of a hundred-foot cliff.

When we arrived at the bottom of the cliff, we geared up and began our climb. My friend was leading the climb up a small chimney crack that led to a rocky outcrop. As we reached the base of the outcrop my friend anchored himself in with carabiners and pitons, reached up to grab the edge of the ledge and began to pull himself up to the vulture's nest.

I'm sure you can guess who was standing on the edge of the nest looking down, MAMA VULTURE!

Martin Tyner

The vulture does not have large, powerful claws like an eagle to defend the nest, and even though a vulture could bite you viciously, that's not how they defend their nest. Vultures have a very special way of defending their nest. They throw up on you.

Imagine looking over to see my friend hanging in space, screaming as this black, chunky ooze flowed down over his head!

Remember vultures consume dead, rotted flesh.

Needless to say, we did not get into the vulture's nest that day. We climbed down the cliff, collected our gear, and started the hour's walk back to the truck in ninety degree heat. By the time we arrived back at the truck, all of the vulture vomit had dried on my friend.

You cannot imagine the smell of vulture vomit: dead, rotted flesh regurgitated. There is nothing on the planet that smells that bad. Compared to vulture vomit a skunk has a pleasant odor. So my friend sat in the back of the truck, and I drove home.

When we arrived at his parent's home, his mother was furious. She had him strip down naked in the garage and ordered him to take a shower as she threw his clothes in the trash. My friend showered and showered and showered, but he could not wash off the smell.

For the entire last month of school, there wasn't a teacher that would let him in the classroom. He had to sit outside the classroom with the door open. There wasn't a girl in my high school that would go out with him for more than a year, and we don't want to go into nicknames, because that's far too cruel.

The reason I tell this story is that I want everyone to know that a bird's nest is a sacred place, a nursery where mom and dad raise their young. When you find a bird's nest, stay back and watch the comings and goings with a pair of binoculars and allow the mom and dad birds to raise their young in peace.

Guardian Angel

Simi Valley, a small agricultural community where I lived, was nestled in a little valley about three miles wide and eight miles long. The surrounding foothills were covered with grass and the occasional live oak tree.

My best friend, Mark, and I decided that we would go over to Chatsworth, which was the next community to the southeast. We wanted to go to a sporting goods store to pick up ammunition for our guns, so that later that week we could do some target practice.

Mark was able to borrow his mother's car, which was a brand new 1975 Chevy Malibu. It was a two-door hardtop, red in color, high-back front bucket seats, and a 350 cubic inch V8 under the hood. For a couple of teenage boys, this was a great ride! It was a big step up from the old 1955 Chevy Pickup we were used to driving.

It was getting late, so after purchasing our ammunition we had to hurry back home to return the car. It was his mother's bowling night. His mother was an avid bowler, and she would shoot us if we made her late.

The road from Chatsworth to Simi Valley was called Box Canyon Road, approximately fifteen miles of steep, hairpin turns that wound its way through the foothills and back into our small valley.

Leaving the sporting good store we were late, and it was already dark. The treacherous road lay ahead of us, and we really needed to make up for lost time. Were we speeding? Not excessively. We both knew Box Canyon Road very well.

Mark was driving, and I was the passenger. The radio was turned up, and we were making good time when all of a sudden the car swerved into the mountainside and ricocheted across the road and off the cliff we went.

There is no way to know how far we fell. The cliff was approximately one hundred and forty feet high. I remember tumbling over, and over, and over. The movement seemed to have stopped as quickly as it had started.

Disoriented and confused I sat there, maybe laid there, in dead silence until I heard a voice. It was Mark saying, "Martin, are you all right?"

I responded, "I think so."

Mark said, "Let's get out of here before the car blows up!"

It was pitch black and just a moment earlier I had been sitting in the passenger side front seat. Now I had no idea what my current position was in relationship to the car. As I felt around with my hands, I could feel some kind of opening, so I pulled myself through the hole and found myself on the ground. As I got to my feet, Mark was climbing out the driver's side window.

We left the car and started to climb up out of the canyon. It was steep and rocky, but the climb somehow seemed effortless.

Once we got up to the highway, we decided to walk toward home. We made it about a mile down the road when we saw a county sheriff coming up from the Simi Valley side. We flagged him down and told him that we had been in an accident.

After just a few minutes of answering questions, other rescue vehicles, fire trucks and ambulances, started to arrive. We got into the sheriff's car and directed them back up to the scene of the accident.

As we arrived at the scene, there were a number of rescue vehicles already there that had come from the Chatsworth side. One of my most vivid memories was when the county sheriff called down to the rescue workers at the bottom of the cliff and said, "What are you doing down there?"

The rescuers' hollered up, "We are looking for the bodies."

Mark and I immediately yelled out, "We're up here. We're okay."

The emergency worker yelled back, "You can't be up there, you're dead!"

Notification was made to Mark's parents so they could come and pick us up. We knew we were dead for sure. His mom's brand new car lay totally destroyed at the bottom of the cliff.

When his parents arrived, they were so grateful to see that we were unharmed that there was no mention of the damaged car. We jumped into his father's car, and they drove us home.

The next morning we got up bright and early and drove up Box Canyon Road to the accident site to see if we could figure out what had happened. That's when the reality of the situation hit us both like a ton of bricks!

The accident was caused by the blowout of a faulty tire. When the tire blew, Mark was unable to turn the corner so we impacted a large rock on the right side of the car, which deflected us across the narrow road and directly off the cliff.

As the car went off the cliff, it rolled to the left and on its initial impact, landed on the passenger side roof on top of a large boulder. Then it continued to roll many times until it came to rest on its side, passenger side down, driver's side up. The passenger's side roof, on impact, collapsed all the way to the floor, crushing the passenger's side front seat. The driver's side stayed pretty much intact.

Now this is the part I can't explain. No, I was not wearing a seat belt. Somehow I ended up being thrown into the back seat, and I made my escape through the back window. As I mentioned earlier, Mark's mother was an avid bowler. Just to make things a little more interesting, there were half a dozen bowling balls rolling around loose in the back seat! Not only did I survive a car falling off a hundred and forty foot cliff, I avoided being struck by flying bowling balls as we tumbled over and over again.

If you believe in guardian angels as I do, then it is obvious that my guardian angel works overtime.

Hired as Curator of Birds of Prey

If ever there was a perfect place for a young boy who loved birds, it was Busch Gardens in Van Nuys, California.

In the 1960's Busch Gardens was a beautiful Beer Garden and Bird Park. Admission was free, and I took every opportunity to beg my parents to leave me at the park while they went shopping around the San Fernando Valley.

As a shy, quiet twelve year old I could wander the park completely unnoticed, surrounded by the animals that I loved, especially the birds of prey. I memorized the names and descriptions of each of the creatures in the park. In some odd way they became my friends. I must have watched the bird show at least a hundred times.

My family never understood my fascination with the park. Every time I would tell them, "Some day I will work here as a zookeeper," my mother would look sternly at me and say, "You have to stop playing with these birds and do something with your life."

I had just turned nineteen years old. In January 1975, with a great deal of determination, I jumped in my car and headed to Busch Gardens. Nineteen was the youngest age they would hire anyone to work at the park. Not knowing who to talk to, or even what to say, I decided to wander the park as I had done so many times in the past, to visit with my friends, the critters, and watch the bird show. I knew full well in my heart that this was where I belonged.

When the bird show ended, I mustered up the courage to walk down front and visit with one of the trainers. I told him that I was a master falconer and that it had always been my wish to work here at the park.

The trainer's name was Bill and he suggested that I walk back to the zoo department offices and speak with the zoo department manager, Mr. Meyers.

As I walked through the park heading for Mr. Meyers' office, my mind was racing. What could I say that would convince Mr. Meyers to hire a nineteen year old kid fresh out of high school?

Yes, I had worked for Animal Actors of Hollywood, working with their big cats, elephants and training their raptors, but I wasn't sure how that would qualify me to work at one the country's premiere bird zoological parks.

When I approached Mr. Meyers' office I opened the door and with as much determination and confidence as I could muster, I asked the secretary if I could visit with Mr. Meyers.

The secretary asked if I had an appointment. I answered, "No, but Bill, the head trainer for the bird show, asked me to speak with Mr. Meyers."

So the secretary introduced me to Mr. Meyers. I walked up, shook his hand, introduced myself, and said, "Bill suggested that I speak with you."

Mr. Meyers asked, "Oh, do you know Bill?"

I said, "Of course, we were just visiting."

Mr. Meyers asked me to sit down and we spent about a half hour talking about my experiences and my qualifications. Now it just happened that Mr. Meyers was looking for a bird of prey curator for the park.

Mr. Meyers suggested that I go to the personnel office at the opposite side of the park and visit with the personnel director, Mr. Allen.

I stood up, shook Mr. Meyers hand, looked him straight in the eye and thanked him for his time, then turned and walked from the office.

Once I was back in the park my heart was pounding with excitement! Was it possible? Could this life long dream come true? Could I be hired as the curator of birds of prey at Busch Gardens?

As I walked across the park, again my mind was racing. I found myself not wanting to be disappointed, talking myself down. "I'm just a nineteen year old kid. This is probably just a stupid dream. Maybe Mr. Meyers just wanted me out of his office."

As I arrived at the personnel office I was almost too scared to go in, doubting myself and afraid of rejection. Then some words started to ring in my ears, words from my grandmother, "I know you, and I know how smart you are and there is nothing that you can't do." So I reached for the door, walked into the personnel office and the secretary asked, "Can I help you?"

Again with as much courage and confidence as I could muster I said, "Yes, Mr. Meyers, the zoo department manager, asked me to come and speak with Mr. Allen the personnel director."

The Secretary asked, "Do you know Mr. Meyers?"

My answer was, "Of course, we were just visiting."

So the secretary escorted me immediately to Mr. Allen's office where I walked up to Mr. Allen, looked him square in the eye and shook his hand and said, "My name is Martin Tyner. Mr. Meyers has asked me to speak with you about the curator of birds of prey position here at the park."

Mr. Allen asked, "So, do you know Doug Meyers?"

And I said, "Of course, we were just visiting."

Mr. Allen asked me to take a seat, and we visited for about a half hour talking about my qualifications and expertise. He asked his secretary to bring me an application. I filled it out on the spot, and I was hired before I left the building.

My next stop was wardrobe, where I was fitted with the official zoo department outfit, including khaki green shirt, khaki green pants and knee-high rubber boots. I would start work on Monday.

You can only imagine how I felt leaving the park that day, curator of birds of prey! There were few moments in my life that were more exciting.

When I arrived back home, I walked in the door and my mother asked me where I'd been all day.

I told her, "I went to Busch Gardens for the day."

She looked at me in that stern way and said, "When are you going to get it through your head that you have to stop playing with these birds and do something with your life?"

I said, "Mom, you are looking at the newest curator of birds of prey at Busch Gardens!"

I don't think she knew what to say.

First Day at Busch Gardens

My alarm clock rang at five in the morning, but that really wasn't necessary, I was already awake. I couldn't sleep because of my excitement. I showered, shaved, had a quick breakfast, and jumped in my car for the twenty minute drive to the park.

I walked into wardrobe, to the locker that had been assigned to me a few days earlier and changed from my street clothes to my work uniform: khaki green pants, shirt and knee high, black rubber boots.

As I left wardrobe I walked across the park. It was a beautiful, calm, clear morning. The sun was rising. A low, dense fog hung over the lake and I could hear the sounds of the birds waking up. I could barely contain my joy.

As I got to the zoo department I walked through a large black metal gate and down the hallway. The first door on my right was the kitchen area where the food was prepared for all the animals in the park, with stainless steel metal counters and sinks, red tile floors, white walls and the largest walk-in refrigerator I had ever seen.

As members of the zoo staff started to congregate for the morning meeting, Mr. Meyers introduced me to the staff and handed out our morning assignments.

I was paired up with old Bill, the oldest member of the zoo department staff. Definitely rough around the edges, he had worked at the park for twenty years. I was told this would be a good opportunity to get my feet wet. We would go out on the motor boat and feed all of the animals on the islands around the lake.

We walked into the refrigerator and grabbed dozens of metal trays full of a wide variety of different kinds of foods. Some trays had fruits and vegetables, other trays had a bird of prey diet called zoo preen. Some trays were full of meal worms and other insects. The trays were lined up in a specific order so as we traveled from island to island we could grab the right tray for the right animals.

When the small, wooden boat was loaded with food, both Bill and I jumped into the boat. We pushed it from the dock and with a couple of good pulls on the starting cord the small outboard engine fired up and we were on our way.

Bill sat at the back, steering the boat. I sat up by the bow so that as we approached the island I could jump off the boat, grab the appropriate trays of food, place them on the island, pick up the old trays, put them back in the boat and push the boat off the island so that we could head to the next feeding station.

Shortly after we left the dock I noticed that Bill was wearing a long, heavy, yellow raincoat and a matching yellow rain hat. Now it's true, it was foggy on the lake, but the sky was clear, there was really no chance of rain, so I asked Bill, "Why are you wearing the raincoat?"

With a big smile on his face Bill said, "The engine frequently splashes water up and the coat helps to keep me dry."

I asked Bill, "Do I need a raincoat as well?"

He answered, "No, you won't be driving the boat."

As we headed out from the dock area onto the open lake, it was cool and foggy, and I felt a true sense of adventure.

I thought to myself, "My first day at the park, my first job."

Then, I noticed that seagulls were everywhere lining the banks of the lake, hundreds of them! I was fascinated! It seemed almost as if on cue that all the seagulls took flight at the same time. They made one large circle around the lake and flew directly over the boat. As I looked up to admire the spectacle of so many beautiful birds in flight they all defecated at once.

The attack was carried out with what could only be described as military precision. Their aim was impeccable, perfect, and spot on! Hundreds of bird poops hurling their way down toward me, splattering every inch of my body and the small boat that we were in.

The next sound I heard was not the roar of the boat motor but the roar of Bill's belly laughter as I was trying to wipe the bird poop off my hair, face and body. Then I heard a sound coming from the shore about twenty feet away and there was the rest of the zoo department personnel laughing so hard they could hardly stand up. I knew I'd been had!

We continued our chores to feed the birds on the islands. It took approximately two hours. Two hours covered in bird poop, two hours looking back at Bill's awful grin and hearing his occasional chuckle.

As we returned to the zoo department dock, we tied down the boat, lifted all the dirty food trays onto the dock and climbed out of the boat. Now it was time to wash the dishes.

I was instructed by Doug, the zoo manager, with a big grin on this face, to head back to wardrobe and pick up some clean clothes, then come back to the zoo department where they had a small locker room for zoo department employees. There I could get a shower and get ready for the rest of my day.

Auggie Busch

Once I was cleaned up, my next job was to feed the animals and clean cages in the hospital. The hospital was a relatively small room, about twenty foot square. At the time there were no sick birds in the room, it was more or less a place to hold animals that did not have a permanent place in the park.

There were a variety of small to medium size parrots, a couple of different kinds of ducks, and a black mynah bird. As I started my work in the hospital I would slide large metal trays out from the holding cages, clean them and return them to the cages.

All of a sudden I heard a voice. "Hello."

The voice was clear and bright, and really didn't sound like a parrot. As I looked around the room there was no one there.

I went back to cleaning cages, and I heard the voice again. "Hello."

Again I looked around the room and no one was there. Then I noticed the mynah bird in the direction that the voice had come from, so I walked over to his cage and I heard the voice again, bright, clear and strong. "Hello."

I thought, *A talking mynah bird, how neat.*

As I approached the cage, the mynah bird sounded off again. "Hello."

This time I returned the greeting. "Hello."

The mynah bird cocked his head to the side and said, "What's your name?"

Please understand, after this morning's episode with the seagulls I knew I was working with a crew of practical jokers. I wasn't going to fall into this trap, so I immediately started searching the room for whoever was playing this latest prank.

I looked behind all the cages, in the closets, under the sink, and in the cupboards. There was no one to be found. I walked back to the mynah bird's cage and as I approached, the mynah bird said,

"Hello."

With a great deal of suspicion I returned the greeting. "Hello."

The mynah bird again said, "What's your name?"

I said, "My name is Martin. What's yours?"

The mynah bird said, "My name is Auggie Busch."

Okay that's it, there had to be somebody hiding in the room, a microphone, speaker or something. So I looked in every closet, cupboard and cage, but after an extensive search, again I found nothing.

I walked back to the mynah bird's cage and as I approached the mynah bird said, "Hello."

I returned the greeting. "Hello."

Again the mynah bird asked, "What's your name?"

I answered, "My name is Martin. What's yours?"

Again the Mynah bird said, "My name is Auggie Busch."

The mynah bird then cocked his head to the side and asked, "Do you want a beer?"

Thinking to myself, *Well I might as well go along with the joke.* I said, "Sure, what have you got?"

The Mynah then answered, "Michelob," and began to sing, "*Roll Out The Barrel!*"

By this point I was laughing so hard that I could hardly stand. I walked out of the hospital into the kitchen area and asked Laura, another zoo department employee, "What's the story with the mynah bird in the hospital room?"

Laura said, "The mynah had been trained for a beer commercial but when Mr. August Anheuser Busch, the president of the company saw the commercial with a little black bird introducing himself as Auggie Busch he was horribly offended. He wanted the bird removed from the park, so the mynah was hidden in the hospital room so as not to offend the president of the company."

A Slice

My basic responsibilities at Busch Gardens were to clean, feed and care for all of the birds at the park, especially the birds of prey. We would often be given special duties such as guided tours for VIPs, tours for elementary school groups and security detail.

One day during our morning meeting I was asked to bring out one of our golden eagles for an elementary school tour group that would be arriving at ten o'clock. I hurried up and got the morning chores done, picked up one of the educational eagles and headed back to the zoo department.

As the children arrived we gave them a tour of the kitchen area, the animal hospital, and the bird house. As the children came out of the bird house they gathered around me near the dock area where I brought a large golden eagle out of his kennel.

The look on the children's faces was of total awe and amazement. I started to give a short talk about the physical characteristics of the golden eagle when I noticed that the eagle was preparing to poop.

An eagle can defecate and drop its waste straight down. This is called a mute. An eagle can also defecate and shoot its waste six feet across a room. This is called a slice. It's totally up to the eagle.

The eagle was on my glove. He was starting to lean forward; this was the sign that I had less than two seconds to point the eagle in the right direction. I had about fifty school children in front of me so I quickly swung the eagle so his tail was facing behind me, not realizing that one of the teachers was in the direct line of fire.

He raised his tail and launched a pint of white and black bird poop, hitting the teacher square on the chin, and then it streaked all the way down the front of her dress. I heard a scream from behind me and immediately realized what I had done. Immediately a roar of laughter came from all of the children as members of the zoo staff escorted the teacher to the nearest restroom to help clean her up.

The rest of the talk went off pretty much without a hitch and the children continued their tour of the park. About a week later we received a thank you from the school which included art work from the children of their favorite part of the tour. Virtually every child drew a picture of my eagle pooping on their teacher. Those pictures were on display at the park for months.

World's Toughest Job Interview

Knowing that Busch Gardens in Van Nuys would be closing in a few months and not wanting to be transferred to Saint Louis, Missouri, or Tampa, Florida; I began applying at a variety of wildlife parks and animal training programs.

I received an invitation to come in for an interview at a big cat ranch called Lions Unlimited. The day of the interview I drove out to Lions Unlimited and sat down with their head trainer. After a short review of my résumé the head trainer said, "Well, I can see you have some big cat and elephant experience, but what interests me the most is that we are looking for a bird guy and that appears to be your strong suit."

"Absolutely," I replied.

He said, "Come with me."

We walked out the back door of his office and into the compound area. I was stunned by the sheer numbers of big cats there on the ranch: hundreds of lions, tigers, cougars, jaguars and one African bull elephant.

We walked over to a large enclosure. Inside the enclosure were half a dozen full-grown male African lions. The trainer unlatched the gate, and we walked into the enclosure. He immediately turned around, stepped out of the enclosure and locked the gate behind him leaving me alone with the lions.

"What are you doing?" I asked.

The trainer replied, "You want to be a lion trainer, there are the lions, go train them."

Immediately I protested, "This is not funny!"

Very seriously he answered, "No it's not. There is a big male coming around behind you on your left. You better do something about it before you get eaten."

I glanced around quickly spotting a small, wooden, stock cane hanging on the fence. I grabbed the cane, turned and then ran toward the lion swinging the cane and yelling, "Hah, Hah!" at the top of my lungs. That lion backed down only to have a second one move in from behind, so I went after him as well.

Understanding that even though these lions weighed about four hundred pounds each, when they were standing on the ground they were about four feet tall. I may have only weighed one hundred and sixty pounds, but at five foot, six inches, as far as the lions were concerned, I was bigger than they were. There was no way with a small, wooden cane that I could hurt one of these big cats, but as long as I was bigger, louder and more aggressive, I knew that I could back them down.

After about ten minutes I had all of the lions backed off and the head trainer said as he opened the gate, "Come on out, you did just fine."

As I exited the compound I was angry and with the wooden cane still in hand I confronted him, "What in the heck was that?"

In his defense he answered, "At most big cat training facilities you will have two to four trainers per cat when you are working with the big cats. Here at Lions Unlimited, it's not uncommon to have four big cats being worked by a single trainer, so if something goes bad, it will go bad very fast. I have to trust my life to my trainers. If you would have panicked I would have gotten you out of there, but you handled yourself well. You have the job."

Rampaging Elephant

Lions Unlimited had a large African bull elephant and occasionally I was asked to assist the elephant trainer in moving the elephant around the compound and helping with the training sessions.

The elephant had some favorite tricks that he would like to play on people. He was a tremendous shot when it came to throwing rocks. Anyone within fifty yards was fair game, if they weren't looking. He would pick up a rock with his trunk and hurl it at you, hitting you every time. At least I never saw him miss.

He had a large tractor tire that he enjoyed playing with, which included throwing it over a twelve-foot fence and then becoming virtually unmanageable until you went around the fence, got his tire and brought it back to him. He would then throw it over the fence again; he loved to watch people fetch tires for him.

One morning we were setting up a movie shoot. The scene was a small group of people who were going to attempt to escape across a river in a small, wooden boat, but the elephant would get to the boat first and destroy it. The scene was being shot down by the river, near the parking area. All employees were notified to move their vehicles to a different parking lot, so their vehicles would not interfere with the movie shoot.

The scene was set, the camera crew was ready and the lighting and sound crews were ready. We walked the elephant into the scene and he ignored the boat. We did everything we could to encourage him to play with the boat. He rocked the boat. Then he sat on the boat and all of a sudden there was a loud crunching sound. That was the trigger, the elephant loved that sound. He got more and more aggressive, crushing the boat, mangling it into little pieces.

When the director called, "Cut," the elephant was not about to stop. He was having way too much fun. All of a sudden he noticed a bright yellow Volkswagen Bug parked about twenty feet away, just out of the scene.

He ran to the little car, started pushing on it with his trunk and rolled it completely over onto its roof. He pushed it around in a circle, rolled it back up on its wheels, then climbed on its hood with his front feet. He flipped it over again trying to break pieces off the little car. We were desperately trying to stop this rampage with no luck. All we could do was to stand by and helplessly watch as he ripped the bumper off the car and began beating the car with its own bumper.

After about a half hour the elephant started to get tired and bored. With a little coaxing we were able to walk him back to his compound.

I don't know who owned the Volkswagen, but could you imagine the conversation he must have had with his insurance company? How would you explain an elephant beating your car to death with its own bumper?

Part Five: Love at First Slice – The Rest of the Story

Feathered Doberman Pinscher

One of the biggest misconceptions that people have about wildlife is that if you raise it from a chick, a bird of prey will become sweet, docile and loving. This is about as far from the truth as you can get. Raptors in the nest are heavily motivated by food, and there was never a truer statement than, "Only the strong survive."

Among many species of birds of prey, competition for food is intense. The most aggressive, violent, loudest, and most obnoxious will generally eat first. When mom and dad return to the nest with food, the battle begins.

As the young chicks grow, the competition becomes fierce. It gets to the point where siblings are knocked from the nest, injured, and sometimes killed while attempting to get their share of the available food. In some nests the violence gets so severe that mom and dad will no longer land at the nest site, but fly by and chuck food into the nest and let the young birds fight it out. The young grow very quickly. Most will become fully grown, as large as their parents, between eight and ten weeks of age. There is a great need for large amounts of food to support their rapid growth during this time.

The young fledge (start to fly) between eight and ten weeks of age. As the young become skilled at soaring, they will follow their mom and dad on hunting trips. As the adults swoop down and catch small rodents, birds or whatever is appropriate for their species, it is common for the young hawks to fly down and violently attack their parents, stealing the food to satisfy their ravenous appetites. After a relatively short few weeks of being beaten and brutalized by their young, mom and dad abandon the juvenile birds and begin their migration.

Now picture yourself as a mama hawk with a young bird that you have raised that not only has no fear of you, but no respect for you either. This leads us to the story of Sierra.

Sierra was a young female Harris hawk stolen from her nest by some teenage boys. Not only was she raised by the teenagers, but she was horribly abused. The abuse was so severe that she ended up with a broken leg. Now we have a large hawk, raised by man, with no fear of man, and abused by man; so she hated humans.

She was taken to a veterinarian, and the vet immediately called the local fish and game. The hawk was confiscated and brought to me. Mending the broken leg was far easier than mending the emotional scars that she carried for the rest of her life.

Martin Tyner

This hawk was so emotionally disturbed that she had no idea what she could and could not hunt. Her favorite thing to hunt was cows; yes, cows!

After her leg had healed I would take her out on the desert to give her exercise. If there was a cow within a mile she would leave my glove, fly across the desert and attack the cow violently. She would attack horses, joggers and farmers on tractors. She was a dangerous and violent creature to work with. Fortunately for me, she never turned that aggressive attitude toward me.

One day Sierra and I were returning from a hunting trip, and I stopped by a local gas-and-goodie store to grab a soda pop. Back then I had a very bad habit of leaving my keys on the floor of the car. As I walked out of the store, I heard a man screaming at the top of his lungs. I looked across the parking lot and saw a man bailing out of my car. I ran to the car and discovered Sierra standing on the ground next to it. I picked her up, opened the door and placed her back on her perch where she normally sat free and unhooded.

I noticed then that the keys had been taken from the floor of the car and placed in the ignition. Obviously the man had tried to steal my car. I don't know if he saw the hawk, did not see the hawk, or saw the hawk and thought it was stuffed. I had no idea what was going through his mind, but if you could only imagine jumping into a strange car, picking up the keys from the floor and placing them into the ignition only to have eight, razor sharp talons puncturing the back of your neck, wings beating against your head and the most awful growl that you have ever heard!

There were quarter-size drops of blood going down the street. I had no doubt he needed stitches, I am going to assume that was the last car he ever tried to steal. My Harris hawk was a beautiful black hawk with red shoulders, red thighs and a large white band in her tail. This was how she got her nickname, "My Feathered Doberman Pinscher."

First Date

People frequently ask me how my wife feels about the birds.

By now you have probably come to the conclusion that I have been doing this for a very long time. At the time I wrote this story I have been a falconer for over forty years. I've been married to my sweet wife, Susan, for over thirty years. So, I have been a falconer far longer than I've been married.

On our very first date I took Susan hunting with my hawk, Old Sierra. As you can tell, I'm a romantic kind of a guy. As we arrived at the flying field, I removed my hawk from the car. As Susan approached, Sierra turned on my glove to face her, spread her wings and growled violently at her. Then, Sierra turned back to face me, lifted her tail and "sliced" on Susan.

Let me clarify this for you. A Harris hawk can lean forward and project its waste approximately six feet across a room, approximately a quarter cup in volume and the smell is quite distinctive. This is called a slice.

That was our first date. Susan married me anyway, so it's her fault. The relationship between Susan and my birds is much the same now as it was then, one of tolerance. It's not like she didn't know what she was getting into!

The Rest of the Story *by Susan Tyner*

Sorry to interrupt. I'm Martin's wife, Susan. For the past thirty years I have seldom let Martin finish a sentence without interruption. So there is no way that I will let him write an entire book without putting in my two cents worth. Let me tell you the rest of the story.

Yes, Old Sierra growled and pooped on me and yet I married Martin anyway, but that was just a small part of the story. On that same first date, Martin took me to the home of a friend of his, Hubert Wells, the owner of Animal Actors of Hollywood.

Martin handed me a baby chimpanzee to hold and I followed Martin and Hubert while they went about doing some chores: moving an African lion to clean his cage and exercising an enormous elephant. As we arrived back at the main compound, the chimpanzee in my arms was replaced with a beautiful cougar cub.

I don't know about you, but for me, that was a first date of a lifetime and I couldn't help but look forward to the next one.

The dates that followed consisted of going with Martin to Busch Gardens where he worked and getting a behind the scenes tour; getting to play with macaws and cockatoos, and watching as he cared for an injured hawk and prepared food for the many animals at the park.

He took me to Cougar Hill Ranch, where I got to see cougars and wolves. I even got kissed by a giant grizzly bear. We took long drives spotting raptors on fence posts and power poles. We went hiking through the hills checking out the native wildlife.

We took trips to the Los Angeles Zoo, San Diego Wild Animal Park, Magic Mountain, and Hogel Zoo. At all of these places they not only let us in for free, but gave us a behind-the-scene, VIP tour!

(These were customary courtesies given to fellow zookeepers.)

Martin took me to Lions Unlimited, a job he took at a movie ranch shortly after our engagement. There I got to meet hundreds of African lions, tigers, leopards, cougars, and a jaguar. In addition to the big cats, I also met a big male African elephant, Egyptian vultures, storks and ostriches.

As you can tell, Martin was no ordinary man. To a young, college-age girl who loved animals, Martin was somewhat of a cross between Dr. Doolittle and Crocodile Dundee.

As a young girl I had often fantasized about having a prince in shining armor riding up on a great, white horse to rescue me. Well, my prince wears khaki shirts and blue jeans, and instead of a white horse, he has a golden eagle.

Mother-in-Law *by Susan Tyner*

Martin said I knew what I was getting into before I married him. With that said, there is always something new and surprising at our house. Let me share a couple of stories with you that definitely wouldn't have happened in a normal home.

For those of you that would like a unique way to scare off your mother-in-law, let me tell you how Martin does it at our house.

After I returned home from a brief stay at the hospital for an illness, my dear mother came to stay with us for a few days to take care of me and our two-month old baby so Martin could return to work.

It was great to have my mom help out while I recovered. One morning, while I rested on the couch in the living room, she began to wash the dishes in the kitchen. She had been in the kitchen for several minutes when I heard her scream and watched her streak past me and straight out the front door.

Although I had been half asleep, I knew in an instant what had happened. Since Martin must feed his birds of prey what they would eat naturally, we keep frozen rats and mice in our freezer. He was in the habit of thawing out dead rodents on the window sill above the kitchen sink.

Having been married to Martin for several years, I'd grown accustomed to the sight of a large, dead rat or a couple of mice thawing out on the window sill. They were always sealed in a clear plastic bag, so nothing to worry about, right?

WRONG!

By now you've guessed the reason for my mother's screams. Yes, it was the large, black rat thawing out on the window sill. She stood out in the yard and protested that she would not enter the house until all of the dead rodents were removed from our home. So I placed the rat into a brown paper bag and hid it from sight and did not tell my mother about the freezer full of dead rodents in the basement.

Critters in the House *by Susan Tyner*

Our house has been home to an amazing variety of wild creatures: deer, coyotes, jackrabbits, cottontails, chipmunks, and prairie dogs. We have given sanctuary to rattlesnakes and king snakes, bats and burrowing owls and of course the hawks, eagles and falcons that Martin loves.

One spring day a local sheep rancher came into our pet shop with a beautiful, two-week-old coyote pup. He explained that he had found a den of coyotes right next to his lambing sheds. To protect his newborn lambs, he felt it was necessary to shoot the adult coyotes and destroy the den. At the opening of the crushed den was a single, live pup. As the rancher looked upon this helpless young coyote he couldn't bring himself to dispose of it so he brought her to us.

Martin may be the expert when it comes to wild animals, but my favorite animals have always been dogs. My best friend growing up was a big Labrador retriever-collie mix named Snuggles.

After graduating from high school, I had two career opportunities. The first was to work at a local grocery store as a cashier; the second was to work at a local dog grooming shop as a bather-brusher, washing dogs for a dollar a dog. As ridiculous as it sounded to my parents, I chose to wash dogs. This choice eventually led us to start our own business, Tyner's Pets and Grooming, where Martin managed the pet shop and I groomed dogs. To this day I still love to groom dogs.

As a dog lover, I accepted this coyote pup with excitement. In addition to grooming dogs professionally, I was also showing dogs

Steve Allred

in conformation and obedience as a hobby. I suddenly had a great idea! Wouldn't it be incredible to have the very first coyote ever to be entered in obedience competitions!

With all of my experience handling dogs, I was sure I could appropriately socialize this pup and train her in basic obedience. I could have her registered as a purebred coyote. As a purebred she would be eligible to enter obedience competitions. I was so sure we could complete her Companion Dog (CD) title, which was the first level in obedience competitions. Wow, the first coyote ever with an obedience title! The excitement at the prospect had me grinning from ear to ear.

Martin had been away picking up supplies for our pet store when the pup arrived. By the time he returned I could hardly wait to tell him about my exciting plans for this beautiful coyote puppy. When Martin returned I began to tell him about my plans. He looked at me and said, "Sue, it's not a dog; it's a coyote!"

My feelings were hurt. Martin just didn't understand. I knew I could socialize and train the coyote pup, I was sure of it. Being stubborn I said, "I know it will be a lot of work, but I know I can do it. I'll show you. You'll see."

Martin just smiled at me. Boy, that made me mad. Now he was laughing at me.

It wasn't long before we had the coyote eagerly feeding on a bottle. Like most wild animals she was heavily motivated by food. Our two children always enjoyed helping us out when it came to bottle feeding baby critters and by the time the coyote arrived in our home, our son, Glen, was a teenager in high school and our older daughter, Vicki, was married and expecting her first baby.

I remember when the coyote was about five weeks old. Glen wanted to feed her so he removed her from the kennel and sat down on the living room floor with the coyote pup in his lap. I handed him the bottle, and the coyote immediately began to feed, tugging and pulling until the bottle was empty. As she began to suck air from the emptied bottle our son pulled it out of her mouth.

As far as the coyote was concerned, our son had just stolen her breakfast, and she was not going to tolerate that. She grabbed his pant leg shaking her head and growling violently. From the kitchen I heard Glen yell, "Mom, the coyote is biting me!"

As he pulled the coyote off his pant leg, he climbed up the back of the couch with the baby coyote in hot pursuit. As I entered the living room I found Glen standing on his left leg on the back of the couch with the coyote dangling from his right pant leg.

I grabbed the pup by the scruff of the neck, and she immediately turned her violent temper toward me, so I quickly put her back in her kennel and closed the door.

It was hard for me to believe that this cute, little, bottle-raised coyote could be so aggressive at such a young age. Martin's words came back to me, "Sue, it's not a dog; it's a coyote!"

Boy, I hate it when he's right!

Communicating with Coyotes *by Susan Tyner*

For the safety of our friends, family and wildlife foundation volunteers, it was time to start treating the young pup as a coyote and not a dog. So, Martin called us all together to give a basic lesson in coyote behavior and etiquette.

Coyotes have a very strong survival instinct called, "fight or flight". This means if a coyote becomes frightened and it cannot run away it will instinctively attack. This is not anger. This is instinct. No matter how tame a wild animal seems to be, the fight or flight instinct is always present.

Coyotes have a very well-defined family structure. A young coyote's job is to establish its ranking within the family unit. This is done by being the strongest and most aggressive (survival of the fittest).

When our son removed the bottle from the coyote pup, she considered that a challenge to her position within the family. Her response was to drive off the competition.

When a young coyote pup gets out of hand then it's mama coyote's responsibility to control the aggression and put the young pup in its place. This is done by pinning the young pup to the ground with her paws, standing over the top of it and giving the pup a threatening growl.

In coyote language this is like a time out or sending a child to their room. The coyote learns that there are boundaries in life and to respect their parents. For the next several months we learned, under Martin's close supervision, that whenever the coyote showed any sign of aggression or dominance, we would immediately respond like a mama coyote with a stern and dominant growl.

This had an unexpected side effect. By now we had a new grandson, Dylan. When Dylan was approximately eight months of age, we received an excited phone call from our daughter, Vicki, who had spent a great deal of time helping us with the coyote. She had great news! Our grandson had just spoken his first words.

Steve Allred

Of course Martin immediately wanted to know, "Was it 'Grandpa'?"

Vicki said, "No."

I asked, "Was it 'Grandma'?"

Again she answered, "No."

"Was it Mom or Dad?"

"No."

"Well, what was his first word?"

Then Vicki explained with a smile in her voice, "We were at Wal-mart today and a woman came up to us and said, "What a cute baby!"

Dylan looked up at the woman, smiled and said, "Grrrrrrr."

Living in Utah *by Susan Tyner*

In the spring of 1982, Martin and I opened Tyner's Pets and Grooming in Cedar City, Utah. Martin managed the pet shop, and I groomed dogs and cats.

As a falconer and a licensed wildlife rehabilitator, Martin was asked to provide bird of prey programs to our local schools and scouts. He enjoyed sharing his knowledge with the children in hopes that they would gain love and respect for these magnificent birds and the environment that we share.

The programs were provided free of charge. As long as they were in our local community, they didn't keep Martin away from work too long. So, I was able to run the pet shop until he returned. After a while, the news spread about how enjoyable, as well as educational these programs were and he began to get requests from neighboring towns and cities. Martin was now traveling throughout the state of Utah and southern Nevada with his raptors.

A small family pet shop doesn't provide a lot of profit, so we'd always driven used vehicles. Traveling in the summer's heat with federally protected wildlife became a concern should the car have a problem, so in 1994 we invested in our first new car: a Geo Metro four-door hatchback with a little three-cylinder engine!

Martin constructed traveling cages for his eagle, hawk and falcon that gave them as much room as possible but would still fit into the small car. These cages were made of lightweight wood with holes drilled along the sides for ventilation. Each contained a carpeted perch inside for the bird to stand on.

Limited resources can inspire creativity. Martin constructed the eagle's travel cage with a top that could be lowered to go through the open hatchback. Once inside the car, the top was raised giving the eagle more head room. This was an economical way to transport the birds to programs.

As Martin traveled further and further providing free raptor programs to schools and scouts, and as the frequency of these programs increased, he began to feel guilty. This was not only taking up his time, but also eating up the limited income our small business provided. It was about this point in time that I suggested he keep providing the local programs for free but he should at least request payment for mileage to cover the gas when he had to travel out of town.

Martin resisted charging for mileage. He loved scouting as a boy and wanted to give back to the scouting program. Also the schools in Utah had limited budgets. I became more persistent, eventually convincing Martin that he could provide all the programs for free, but anything out of town we would have to charge something to cover our mileage.

This got us by for a few more years but it was amazing how fast he put a hundred thousand miles on that little car, and we had not even finished paying it off. The prospect of purchasing a new vehicle while still owing on the last was frightening. At the same time, our house needed a new roof as well as painting.

In the pet shop we raised as many of our own animals as possible; from canaries, cockatiels and parakeets to guinea pigs, hamsters, rabbits, rats and mice. We had been increasing the number of mice and rats we raised for several years in order to feed the ever increasing number of injured and orphaned birds of prey that arrived on our doorstep, as well as Martin's falconry and educational birds. We were also paying employees to keep the shop running while

Martin was away providing more programs.

In addition to providing falconry programs all summer long for the Utah Shakespearian Festival, Martin traveled during the school year providing school programs as far as Phoenix, Arizona, and the New Mexico Military Institute. He loved providing raptor programs to enthusiastic children and adults as well, but the guilt he felt for taking time and resources away from his family put a constant stress on him until it became overwhelming.

The Gift of Love *by Susan Tyner*

One evening in the late summer of 1997 Martin asked me out to a quiet dinner. It was nice, just the two of us after a long day at work. Martin loved to hold my hands and look into my eyes across the table. He can be very romantic and that evening it especially touched me that even after nineteen years of marriage he still told me how much he loved me and how lucky he was to have me and our two beautiful children.

This particular evening though, after sharing those sentiments, he started to tear up. He told me that he was going to give up falconry, give up wildlife rehabilitation, and give up providing educational outreach programs. Although he loved to provide them, he felt so much guilt about what he wasn't providing for his family that it was eating him up inside.

He loved us so much that he was willing to give up everything else so he could give his family more. He would be available to work in the pet shop full time again, so we wouldn't have to pay employees while he was away providing programs and caring for the wildlife. We wouldn't spend as much money feeding the injured and orphaned critters, and we wouldn't put so many miles on our vehicle so the car would last longer.

He thought he had it all figured out; his wife and children deserved better, they deserved more. I listened to him carefully as silent tears rolled down my face, and my heart swelled with love for my husband.

I looked Martin in the eyes and said, "I love you, but I can't let you stop. You have been given a very special gift, a calling. You have the ability to care for God's sick, injured and orphaned creatures. You understand them. You know what they are going to do before they do it.

"You are a healer and a teacher. You make a difference in people's lives. You are passionate about what you do and that has always been something I've loved about you. I don't need a fancy house or fancy possessions. I have much more than most people will ever understand. I have your friendship and your love, that is something that money cannot buy."

The Southwest Wildlife Foundation *by Susan Tyner*

The next day I made an appointment with our business accountant, Stephen Strand. I asked for his help to start a non-profit organization so we could accept donations to help offset the cost of travel and feed for the injured wildlife.

His response was, "What took you so long? I was wondering when you were going to do this!"

Martin and I could not have started a 501c3 non-profit organization on our own and I am grateful to Stephen and Kathy Strand, not only for their expertise, but for their enthusiasm and generous donation of time in helping us found the Southwest Wildlife Foundation.

Too Dumb to Quit

The Southwest Wildlife Foundation, Inc. is a non-profit organization dedicated to the care and rehabilitation of native wildlife and to provide wildlife and environmental educational programs to schools, scouts and other community events throughout the west.

As the number of wildlife rescues and educational programs began to grow, it was natural that our board of directors would look into the possibility of acquiring property to give the foundation a permanent home. We looked at a number of properties around the

Southern Utah area. Although several pieces of ground would have been appropriate for a nature park, the Coal Creek property was one of the best opportunities. Twenty-three acres of ground along Highway 14, a mile and a half east of the center of town where an old, coal-fired power plant once stood.

The power plant was decommissioned and disassembled over twenty years ago. The ground was abandoned with remnants of coal ash throughout the property, basically a low-grade, toxic waste dump. This was a place for the wayward high school and college kids from the community to party, and buy and sell drugs. It was an abandoned piece of ground torn up by motorcycles and ATVs. It was a place where people would illegally dump their trash.

The ground was so much more! Even with all of its abuse, the ground still maintained an unexpected natural beauty. It was nestled between two beautiful, red Navajo sandstone mountains with an old Civilian Conservation Corps drop structure which formed a beautiful waterfall as Coal Creek flowed through the center of the property. You could walk from the sage brush, through pinion and juniper forest, down to the cottonwoods along the stream, and up to ponderosa pines at the top of the mountain.

This property had an indescribable appeal that seemed to draw me close. I saw in this ground, that sat upon the transition point between the Colorado Plateau and the Great Basin, a vision of its potential. I could visualize the property improving the quality of life for the residents of Southern Utah. It would be a place to teach and develop an understanding and respect for Utah's native wildlife and their habitat. It would be a place to care for the sick, the injured and the orphaned wild creatures that call Southern Utah their home.

The decision was made by the board of directors to approach Utah Power to see if they would be willing to donate this ground for the creation of a permanent wildlife rescue facility and a nature park for the children of Utah.

This idea was met with a great deal of skepticism from people in the community. To the best of anyone's knowledge, Utah Power had never donated property to anyone and it seemed very unlikely that a small, volunteer wildlife group would have any chance at all of acquiring some of the most valuable commercial property in Iron County.

Susan Tyner

Now it was time to ask for the property. With the support of my wife, Susan, and with no prior experience, we attempted to write a grant. No one believed it was possible, not Utah Power, not Cedar City, not even our board of directors, but we submitted our first grant request anyway, and the process was started.

After about a year of meetings, letters and phone calls (much to Utah Power's credit, they never said no), they told me that we would really have to deal with their parent company, Pacificorp, in Portland, Oregon. Truth be known, I think they were getting tired of me.

After another year of meetings, letters and phone calls (again much to Pacificorp's credit, they never said no), I was told that Pacificorp/Utah Power was being sold to Scottish Power and that we would have to deal with Scotland.

By this time I don't know if we caught the sympathy of many of the good people at Utah Power or their respect, but the local people of Utah Power really went to bat for us. I asked and was given an opportunity to make a five-minute presentation to one of Scottish Power's Vice Presidents as he traveled through the states surveying what they had just purchased.

In the spring of 2000 on a bright sunny day, I met with the Vice President of Scottish Power and his people. I had an architectural concept drawing of the park and did my very best to describe the value of this ground to the people of Utah and why this was the perfect place for the nature park.

The Vice President of the company was kind and patient and listened to what I had to say, but I could see in his eyes that I really wasn't getting anywhere. There was no reason for Scottish Power, a large international corporation, to donate millions of dollars worth of property to a small, wildlife rescue group in Iron County, Utah.

I stated to the Vice President of Scottish Power, "I have a friend that I would like you to meet."

He asked, "Who's your friend?"

I said, "I have brought a live eagle for you to meet."

He asked, "Is it a golden eagle?"

I said, "Absolutely!"

In Scotland, there was a sense of national pride with the reintroduction of the golden eagle back to Scotland, very much like the bald eagle here in the United States. He said, "I must get my camera!"

We spent the next fifteen minutes doing a photo shoot with the Vice President of Scottish Power and my golden eagle, Bud.

At the end of the photo shoot the Vice President of Scottish Power reached over, shook my hand and said, "I don't know what it takes in the States to do this, but you have your property."

A few more months of paperwork and then the good news finally arrived. The property was ours!!!

There are still people to this day that shake their head and wonder how we convinced Utah Power/Scottish Power to donate this property. I tell them that they should never underestimate the power of a golden eagle and a human that is too dumb to quit.

Blessings and Prayers

With the amazing gift from Utah Power of twenty-three acres of beautiful canyon property for the purpose of wildlife rescue and wildlife education, we felt it would be very appropriate to invite the community out for a property dedication ceremony.

Because this ground was once Paiute ground (the Paiutes are the native people of southern Utah), we wanted to invite the Paiute spiritual leader to come and assist us with our property dedication and blessing of the ground. We found this process to be a little more complicated than one would imagine, for the Paiute people tend to be a shy, quiet people with deep spiritual and cultural roots. They consider their religion, language and lifestyle to be sacred.

We asked and were given the opportunity to present our request before the Cedar Paiute Clan at their council meeting. We were told that they would let us know once the Council had made a decision.

When the word came back from the Council, we were told that Mr. Clifford Jake, the Paiute spiritual leader, had been given permission from both the Cedar Clan and the Indian Peaks Clan to participate in blessing the ground. We were also told that because the Paiute people considered their language sacred, the blessing would be done as a prayer or a whisper. It was a tremendous honor to have Mr. Jake participate in the property dedication!

On the morning of November 11, 2000, we woke up to bright blue skies, temperatures hovering around zero and two feet of snow on the ground. It was unusually cold for the first part of November. We were afraid that few people, if anyone, would show up for the property dedication. Much to our surprise, approximately a hundred people from the community braved the bitter cold to share in what could only be described as a once in a lifetime opportunity.

Mr. Jake arrived with his grandson. He stepped out of the pickup truck. He was a small, slender man in his eighties. With the help of his grandson, he walked through the snow to the area where the blessing was to be performed.

The crowd fell silent as they saw Mr. Jake approach. There was a great reverence, mixed with anticipation, as Mr. Jake spoke. He requested that we stand in a large circle and that the circle should open to the east, forming a large horseshoe. The ground in the center had been prepared by removing the snow so that the blessing could be done on bare ground.

Mr. Jake took his place in the center of the prayer circle. He carefully laid out a Native American blanket and set a small, wooden box; a small, stoneware pot; and a juniper branch upon the blanket. He asked that no pictures or movies be taken, for the blessing was sacred. He asked his grandson to start the chant music and he bent down and opened the wooden box and removed from the box his eagle feathers.

The eagle feathers were fastened in the shape of a small fan. He picked up the small pot and the juniper branch and carefully lit the juniper branch, blew out the flame and set the smoking branch in the small pot that he held in his left hand. With the eagle feather fan that he held in his right hand, he would fan the smoke, and with absolute silence Mr. Jake began his prayers.

Once he finished his prayers he asked me to step forward into the prayer circle. As I approached, Mr. Jake asked me, "Is your eagle here today?"

I said, "Of course, Bud (my golden eagle), is with me."

He then asked, "Can you bring the eagle into the prayer circle?"

I brought my golden eagle to the center of the prayer circle, placed him on a perch and then stepped back.

As quickly as I stepped back, Mr. Jake began his prayers a second time, blessing the ground and blessing my eagle as well. I was later told that this was the first time in his eighty plus years that he had the opportunity to perform a blessing with a live eagle.

Mr. Jake requested that I enter the prayer circle a second time and as I approached he asked that I stand in his place and face the east. As I took his place in the center of the prayer circle, he moved to my left and began his prayers a third time, blessing the ground, blessing my eagle and blessing me as well.

This time, all of the words in the prayers were spoken in a voice loud enough so that I could hear the prayers. I was surprised and very honored that he would share his language with me, though I do not speak Paiute and could not understand the prayers.

When Mr. Jake finished his prayers he placed his hand on my shoulder and spent the next several minutes explaining to me what each of the prayers meant. He then left my side and quietly shook the hands of everyone in attendance. Just before he left, he asked if I would please come to his home.

Healer of Angels

When the dedication ceremony was over I felt drawn by Mr. Jake's invitation to visit his home. Though I have driven by his home on a number of occasions — he lives just a few blocks from me — I've never had the opportunity to sit down and visit with him for any length of time. As I pulled up to his house, his grandson met me at the door and very warmly invited me in.

As we sat down in the living room, Mr. Jake entered the room from the hallway and took his place on the couch next to me. He was pleased with the way the dedication ceremony had gone and appreciated the reverent way everyone responded. Then, Mr. Jake proceeded to tell me the story of the eagle.

He said, "To the Paiute people, the eagle was once human. The most noble and courageous of the native people was asked by the Great Spirit to come and sit in Council in Heaven.

"This noble and courageous brave answered the Great Spirit by saying, 'I cannot sit in Council in Heaven, because I cannot fly.' So the Great Spirit turned him into an eagle, and the eagle was given a calling.

"The eagle was to remain upon earth by night to collect all of the prayers from the People of the Nation, and then by day he was to ride the currents of warm rising air up to Heaven and deliver the prayers to the Great Spirit. He was then to receive all of the blessings from the Great Spirit and deliver those blessings to the People of the Nation."

Mr. Jake went on to say, "To a Paiute person, when they see an eagle flying overhead, they believe that eagle is one of the Great Eagles, and that the eagle is watching over them and their family personally, like a guardian angel."

When he finished the story I thought, what a wonderful explanation as to why the native people believe the eagle is sacred.

Mr. Jake then said, "In the Paiute culture, when you receive your first blessing, it is customary for you to receive a Paiute name."

I'll be honest with you, I was a little nervous, I'm not really the *"Dancing with Wolves"* type. Though I have great love and respect for the Paiute people and their culture, I did not know what to expect as far as receiving a name.

The name that I was given was "Poown'hunt Kwuwnunts." The closest English translation for "Poown'hunt" would be *"healer or spiritual doctor"* and "Kwuwnunts" which means *"eagle."*

Mr. Jake then went on to explain that because of all of the eagles that I have cared for in my life and returned to the wild, and eagles are the guardian angels of the Paiute people, that I am to be know as "Healer of Eagles" or "Healer of Angels." He told me that I have a sacred calling to protect the ground of the nature center and that the ground is to remain sacred for the healing of angels and all of Utah's wildlife.

A few years later Mr. Jake passed away. At his funeral they spoke of Mr. Jake and how someday he will return as one of the Great Eagles to watch over the Paiute people. After the funeral was over, a very kind elderly Paiute woman approached me and asked, "Mr. Tyner, if you ever have the opportunity to care for Clifford Jake, would you please let us know?"

Steve Allred

Part Six: A Promise is a Promise

A Childhood Fantasy

I've always believed that we have come to earth with a mission in life. I've always believed in a pre-existence, a God, a Father, a Great Spirit. I've always believed that we are children of nobility, that we have left the comforts of a heavenly existence to come to earth to learn, to teach, to experience, and to honor our promises and commitments. I believe we made promises to each other, to help one another through the trials, pains, and hardships that can occur here on earth.

Though we may have no memories of our previous life, we frequently will receive small promptings, a gentle guidance that will help steer us in the direction that our lives are meant to go. Often these promptings are no more than a childhood fantasy or a gentle heart's desire that seems to reoccur.

One of my greatest childhood fantasies was the desire to create a personal friendship with a wild eagle. I found myself with a love and fascination for these powerful creatures.

One day I found a book called *Falconry* by Humphrey ap Evans. Although not my favorite falconry book, there is one photograph of a large, burly, Russian falconer with his golden eagle and a collection of European brown hares that the eagle had caught.

I don't know why that particular photograph so sparked my imagination, but I found myself frequently dreaming of one day wandering the deserts with an eagle as he soared the skies. With a gentle whistle, my friend — my eagle friend — would return to my glove.

By this time in my life I was a shy, dyslectic teenager, spending all of my time wandering the foothills of Southern California and taking every opportunity to check out books on falconry at the local library.

My parents were getting concerned and would frequently say, "You need to stop playing with birds and do something with your life." So I would put my dreams on hold, and try to come back to reality.

Making a Dream Come True

Twenty years have passed. I now have a wife, a family, a job; but for some reason my childhood dream, the idea of developing a personal friendship with a wild eagle, would never leave. I guess this sounds ridiculous, at least it did to most.

"It's impossible, you can't have a golden eagle; they're federally protected."

No one understood that more than I.

By now most of my life was dedicated to the rescue, rehabilitation, and release of injured wildlife, including eagles. All of the animals that came into rehabilitation were to be returned to the wild and there was a deep need to maintain an emotional distance so that they would not bond to humans. Nevertheless my childhood desire would just not go away.

I started a personal quest to legally acquire a golden eagle for falconry, which everyone knew was impossible.

I first contacted the U.S. Fish and Wildlife Service, and I received a resounding "NO" from the director of Region Six. I believe his exact words were, "You will never have an eagle for falconry, not in this lifetime or the next!"

This was followed by a similar response from the Utah Division of Wildlife Resources.

Now I've never been very good at taking "No" for an answer. With a strong moral sense of obeying the laws of the land, I knew that I would have to change the laws before I could begin my quest, and this was going to take time.

I responded to this challenge by requesting justification from both the U. S. Fish and Wildlife Service and the Utah Division of Wildlife Resources and received a laundry list of reasons why eagles may not be used for falconry.

I took the list as a guideline and started to address each of their points of concern. This process took over four years! Four years of "No!" for an answer. I would request justification, meet those requirements and then reapply.

I repeated this process so many times that finally both the U.S. Fish and Wildlife Service and the Utah Division of Wildlife Resources ran out of No's.

Here is the short list of what it took for me to legally acquire a golden eagle for falconry.

First, I must be a falconer.

To become a falconer you must read every book on falconry that you can find. There is a written test that you must pass and the test is administered by the State Fish and Game. Like most government tests, the test was extensive and badly written.

Once you've passed the written test, you must have your facilities inspected to make sure you have all that you need to care for the birds properly. Then you must apprentice for two years under a general class or master class falconer. At the end of your two years' apprenticeship there will be a variety of hawks and falcons that you may have for falconry, but you may not have an eagle.

It takes five more years before you can apply for a master class falconry license.

Now it did not matter that I was a master falconer with twenty years' experience flying a wide variety of hawks and falcons. That still did not qualify me to fly a seven pound golden eagle.

The U. S. Fish and Wildlife Service required that I have two years' experience flying eagles before they would give me a permit to fly eagles, and of course I could not fly an eagle without a permit.

As a federally licensed wildlife rehabilitator who specialized in the rescue and release of injured eagles, I had over ten years experience working with eagles, exercising them and returning them to the wild. That more than met the requirement for the two years of eagle experience, but then I was notified that I must have a one year apprenticeship under an established eagle falconer.

Fortunately, the falconer that trained me was an elderly, multi-generational Hungarian falconer. He had flown eagles throughout Europe and Africa for many years. This allowed me to meet the final requirements to become an American Eagle Falconer.

That was the half-way point. After all of that, I now had to acquire an eagle.

Act of God

There are only two ways that someone can legally acquire an eagle for falconry.

First, the U. S. Fish and Wildlife Service gives you an eagle. Let's say for example, a young eaglet has been stolen from its nest. Hopefully, whoever stole the young eaglet would be caught and convicted, then spend many years in jail, for it's a federal crime.

If a young eagle is raised by man (imprinted), then it has no fear of man. An imprinted eagle released to the wild could seek out civilization and could be a threat to small pets. So, that eagle may be given to a falconer as long as he promises not to hunt the bird around his neighborhood.

The second way to legally acquire an eagle for falconry is to trap a full grown wild eagle that has been classified as a depredation bird (a threat to livestock).

First there must be a rancher who considers an eagle a threat to his livestock. Then I would have to convince the rancher, "Please do not shoot the eagle. Let me see what I can do." Unfortunately, eagles do get shot.

Next, I would have to convince the U. S. Fish and Wildlife Service, the Utah Division of Wildlife Resources and the U. S. Department of Agriculture that it would be in the eagle's best interest to remove him from the potentially life threatening situation and have the eagle available, not only for falconry, but for my wildlife educational programs.

As I tell everyone, "To have an eagle for falconry is truly an act of God, for I had to get three government agencies to agree on the same thing at the same time." After four years I became the first person in North America to achieve that minor miracle.

Depredation Eagle

Once all of the licenses and permits were issued, I was also issued a government agent who had to be with me throughout the entire trapping process. We then set out to rescue a young male golden eagle that was in a depredation situation.

Working very closely with the agent from the U. S. Department of Agriculture, Animal Damage Control, we set up a bait station in the area where the rancher was concerned about an eagle feeding on his newborn lambs. It took about a week for the eagle to come to the bait station and with great care I was able to trap him and remove him from the situation.

I am often asked, "How do you trap a full grown wild eagle?"

My response is, "Very carefully! Since I am one of few people in North America licensed to trap a wild eagle, I will not go into details, for we do not want people to try this without the proper licenses and permits."

The day was at hand, it was six o'clock in the morning. The sun was starting to rise over the mountains to the east. I was about two miles to the west of the bait area on a small rise surrounded by pinion and juniper forest with a spotting scope fixed on the bait station. We watched the surrounding areas for any sign of the offending eagle.

Suddenly, a dark figure landed at the top of a power pole approximately a hundred yards from the bait station. It was the eagle that we'd been watching for days, and he was showing great interest in the lamb carcass at the bait station.

The young eagle surveyed the surrounding area and when he felt it was safe he glided down to feed on the carrion meal we had provided for him. After just a couple of minutes the eagle jumped vertically into the air, and my first thought was, *Maybe we've got him.*

He jumped a second time and attempted to fly but could only fly about ten feet when he was gently pulled back to the ground.

I grabbed my spotting scope, threw it into the truck and with the agent from the USDA, ADC sitting next to me, I raced down the small dirt road as fast as my small pickup could go in first gear. I was so excited, I forgot to shift.

I slammed on the brakes, jumped from the truck and somehow I flew over a five-foot high, barbed wire fence. I ran two hundred yards across the open field and tackled the eagle. Once getting control of his feet and tucking him under my arm, I could then remove him from the trapping equipment. We walked back across the field to my truck where, on the tailgate I gave the eagle a thorough inspection. I found him healthy and unharmed, but like all eagles that I rescue, horribly infested with lice.

I gently placed a hood over his head to help reduce his stress and then placed him in a large airport kennel. It was time to go home, outfit the eagle with his falconry equipment and start the gentling process called "manning."

A Falconer's Wake

This was where all of my experience as a wildlife rehabilitator, rescuing eagles, ended. All of the wild eagles up to this point I would never gentle. My job was not to become their friend, but to care for their injuries or illnesses and return them to the wild as quickly as possible.

I was the one that was frequently called to chase down the injured eagles and capture them, bringing them into captivity. I would put in stitches, take out stitches, inject them with medications, push feeding tubes down their throats and subject them to physical therapy; preparing them for the day they could be returned to the wild.

When the eagles are returned to the wild they don't like me, and that's wonderful. Hopefully, they will stay far away from humans.

It was now time for the master falconer to take over, to gentle and befriend the wild eagle. My childhood dream had just begun. I named the eagle "Bud." As Bud and I traveled home my mind was awhirl with childhood thoughts and fantasies. Even though I knew the reality was, this was a wild eagle! He would never be, and should never be, considered a pet.

When we arrived home, the first order of business was to get the eagle outfitted with leather anklets and leather straps called jesses and bring him down into the basement where it was cool and dark.

I called my wife, Susan, and let her know that Bud was now home and that I was planning a traditional falconer's wake, would she please bring home lots of videos and munchies. A wake is when a falconer stays awake with the bird until the bird becomes calm and eats.

The basement was dark with the only light coming from a small television across the room with the sound turned down low. The eagle was sitting on my right arm. I could feel the power of his talons restricting the blood flow through my thick, double-layered leather glove. I gently reached over and loosened the ties on the hood and with my slightest movement the eagle suddenly clamped down and was crushing my arm.

I slowly and gently removed the hood and in the darkness of the room, Bud and I sat virtually nose to nose, or beak to beak (whichever you prefer), as this beautiful, wild, frightened creature tried to understand what was happening to him.

We sat in the dark all day, as I gently touched his feet, stroked his breast, his head and back. Speaking calmly and gently, using all of my skills to assure him that he wasn't going to be harmed, in the hopes that soon he would reach down and feed on a jackrabbit leg

I held between the fingers of my gloved hand.

We sat quietly for three days and three nights. Finally Bud reached down and began to feed from my glove. This was a major milestone in our relationship. He started to realize that his life wasn't in danger, accepting my touch and even acknowledging that the preening felt good.

Training an Eagle

The next step was to take Bud out to his house, which was called a "mews." His mews was a building that was eight feet high, ten feet wide, and sixteen feet long. It was equipped with perches and bath pans for his comfort.

Every day I would go out to his house, and I would bring him goodies: jackrabbit, quail, pigeons, rats, and mice. You see, the way to an eagle's heart was through his stomach. Bud learned very quickly that his captivity was not so bad. He looked forward to my visits and enjoyed our social time together.

Susan Tyner

One day I did the most awful thing. I walked into his house with food on my glove and said, "Good morning Bud, I have your breakfast." In typical eagle fashion, Bud gave me a look which said, "Bring it here."

I said, "Bud, in order for you to get your breakfast you must step from the perch to my glove, and I will feed you."

Wow, if looks could kill, I would be dead! He stomped his feet, beat his wings, and screamed violently at me. Let me assure you there is no two-year old child on God's green earth that can throw a tantrum quite like a wild golden eagle!

As any good parent would do, I calmly said, "When your tantrum is over, you still must step to the glove before I will feed you." With a little patience and persistence, he stepped up to the glove and began to feed.

The next day we extended the distance to a foot, and then three feet, six feet, ten feet, to the length of his house. Soon he was outside and flying the length of the backyard.

Then came the day that all falconers fear. I took my eagle back to the desert, to a place very similar to the area he came from. I removed his equipment, unhooded him, cast him off my arm, and let him fly free; with the hope that when I blew my whistle, he would turn back and land on my glove for food.

The entire process that I have just described took approximately a month.

Eagle on Welfare

My childhood dream was now a reality. I had my friend, Bud, the golden eagle, who would soar the skies and then at the sound of my whistle, would return to my glove. We would go for wonderful evening walks.

As the sun sank low in the sky and the clouds turned a beautiful crimson red, Bud and I would wander though the desert. He would fly from a fence post, to sage brush, to a hillside and then back to my glove. It was a time of calm reflection and an almost spiritual connection, a walk with one of God's most perfect creatures.

Nevertheless, we had a problem. I had a golden eagle on welfare. It was time for Bud not only to fly like an eagle, but to hunt like an eagle. It was time to reintroduce Bud to live quarry.

This may be hard for some to understand. An eagle's job in life is to hunt jackrabbits and to help prevent the overpopulation of large rodents. As a wildlife rehabilitator, I raised rats, mice, rabbits, quail and pigeons to feed the sick, injured and orphaned raptors we cared for.

I headed out to the desert with Bud on one of our normal evening walks. Just before getting Bud out of the truck I picked up a small, wild-looking rabbit that was ready to be butchered as food for the injured raptors we cared for. I placed the rabbit under a bush and marked the bush with a soda pop can so I could remember where the rabbit was. I returned to the truck to pick up Bud, and we started our evening walk.

Bud left my glove and flew to the top of a hill. With a whistle, he would come flying back to my glove for a bit of food and then off again to a fence post, and then back to the glove for another treat.

As we approached the bush marked by the soda pop can, Bud immediately spotted the rabbit. Remembering that he was an eagle, Bud dashed from the glove, caught the rabbit and killed it instantly. I moved in quietly and picked up Bud along with the rabbit he had just caught and killed. He ate all that he wanted and then we went home to butcher out the rest of the rabbit to feed to the other injured raptors we were currently caring for.

The next time we went afield, I took a second wild-looking rabbit. I placed the rabbit under a bush, then marked the bush with a soda pop can and returned to the truck for Bud. As we started our evening walk, Bud stood tall on the glove, spotted the soda pop can fifty yards away and immediately left the glove, crashed through the brush and caught the rabbit.

Eagles are so incredibly smart! Bud recognized the soda pop can.

Our training was over, there was nothing left to do but enjoy our friendship and bond closer. We would go hunting four to five times a week. Bud would leave my glove and fly up to the ledges. There he would use the ridge lift to gain altitude, often times flying with the wild eagles.

A Good Dog

I am frequently asked, "If the eagle is allowed to fly free, why does it come back?"

An eagle, like all birds of prey, is an intelligent opportunistic predator. Just like you and me, he is always looking for the easiest meal. This is why McDonald's and Burger King work so well. There are no fast food restaurants that cater to wild eagles, so they have to be a little more creative.

Though a golden eagle is a large and powerful hunter, a major portion of its diet is road kill deer and rabbits. A dead jackrabbit does not run nearly as fast as a live one. In fact, the number one injury to golden eagles in Southern Utah is being hit by cars as they feed on road kill.

An eagle will take every opportunity to eat as much as it can hold, even to the point of not being able to fly, because it doesn't know where or when its next meal will come from. This makes them vulnerable to speeding trucks and cars. Drivers assume that large birds feeding in the middle of the road will simply fly away. Unfortunately, more often than not, they can't.

So please, if you see a large bird in the middle of the road, slow down and give them the opportunity to get off the road. You'll save an eagle's life and the windshield of your car.

Sorry, back to the original question, why does my eagle come back?

As I said, eagles are intelligent, opportunistic predators looking for the easiest meal.

Imagine this: Bud and I are walking in the desert, and I release him to the sky. He will fly over the ridges north of town, climbing hundreds and sometimes thousands of feet overhead. As I look up into the sky, I frequently see my eagle soaring with other eagles. I often wonder what they must be talking about.

To see my eagle soaring with his friends, I can just imagine him looking over at his buddies and saying, "Watch this, I have a trained human. All I have to do is drift out over that guy's head, and he will run out through the desert with a stick hitting bushes, flushing out rabbits for me to catch. If there are no rabbits to be found I will land on his glove, and he will feed me anyway."

The truth of the matter is that my eagle is the hunter and I am his dog, and I'm a really good dog, so he keeps me.

The Mind of a Jackrabbit

I am frequently asked, "Have you ever been injured by your eagle?"

The answer is, "Yes."

One afternoon Bud and I were out on one of our hunting trips. The weather was perfect. Cool, with a slight south breeze, perfect for soaring the ridges north of town.

As Bud left my glove and flew to the ridge, the air currents immediately lifted him up and he rose higher and higher into the sky.

It was time to get to work flushing jackrabbits for Bud. Occasionally, jackrabbits were few and far between, and this day was such a day. I traveled a good distance beating the brush, and there were no rabbits to be found. Bud had been in the sky for about two hours, and it was time to go home.

When there were no rabbits to be found, I would blow my whistle and throw out a large leather sack with food tied to it. This was called a lure. Bud would dive vertically at a speed of approximately one hundred and forty-five miles an hour and kill the leather sack, which was convenient. I could also blow my whistle, and Bud

Martin Tyner

would fly back and land on my glove for food.

On one particular day Bud got a little confused. He was a thousand feet in the sky, and there were no rabbits to be found. I blew my whistle and threw his lure onto the ground. Bud went into a wonderful dive, headlong, vertical, one hundred and forty five miles an hour. It was impressive, but it was also apparent he wasn't going for the lure; he was coming for my arm.

When I woke up, I was six feet back, laying face down in the dirt with my eagle standing next to me, looking down at me as if to say, "Why are you lying there?"

I had a long talk with Bud that day about how I could not withstand the impact of a seven pound eagle at a hundred and forty-five miles an hour, and I would appreciate it if he would not do that again. He dislocated my shoulder and wrenched my back and knee.

That experience has given me knowledge. You see, I have a knowledge that none of you have: an absolute knowledge of exactly what is going through the mind of a jackrabbit just before an eagle kills him. I don't recommend having that experience, but the knowledge is mine.

Eagle Ambassador

Although Bud was a wild eagle that flew free and hunted like an eagle, he had a second job in life, and that was to be a wildlife ambassador for the Southwest Wildlife Foundation. Bud and I traveled to schools, scout groups and community events throughout the Western United States teaching people about eagles and the environment we share.

It always amazed me to see the level of trust that Bud had in me. He seemed to know that as long as he was on my glove, no harm would come to him. Whether we were performing at the Utah Shakespearean Festival or an auditorium filled with five hundred elementary school children, he displayed a sense of calm and gentle strength.

After many years of wildlife programs Bud seemed to look forward to the activity. With a mischievous sense of humor, he would create opportunities to distract my concentration and focus my attention, as well as everyone else's in the room, on him.

One of his favorite tricks was to reach into my left shirt pocket, grab my glasses and throw them out into the audience. Then he'd look at me with a mischievous look in his eyes, almost as if to say, "Remember, I am the star of the show."

The general public was never allowed to touch or to hold him; he was a wild eagle. Though on rare occasions when I had an individual in the audience who was blind, I would bring them back after the show and with careful instruction they were given the opportunity to see a live eagle with their hands, and Bud seemed to understand.

Sixteen years and over a thousand children's programs, Bud's life touched the hearts of millions.

Eagle Scout Court of Honor

The Boy Scout Eagle Court of Honor is one of my favorite programs. The opportunity to bring a live eagle to participate and honor some of our finest young men who have earned the rank of "Eagle Scout" has always been one of my passions and priorities.

One Eagle Court of Honor stands out in my mind. It was a hometown Court of Honor where fifteen boys received their Eagle Award the same night. Let me be honest, large Eagle Courts of Honor are not a lot of fun and this one was no exception. Fifteen boys meant fifteen families and fifteen groups of friends, hundreds of people in attendance. Often an individual scout can get lost in the crowd.

The program usually starts with an opening prayer and a flag ceremony, a tribute to each of the boys by their parents, then just before the boys receive their Eagle Award, it's our turn. Bud steps onto my glove as he comes out of his kennel. We walk to the front of the room and begin our talk.

"My name is Martin Tyner and this is 'Bud', a full grown wild golden eagle. Scouting has chosen the 'Eagle' to represent its highest award and for some very good reasons. But before I get started on my talk tonight, I have a favor to ask.

"When the Court of Honor is over and you have an opportunity to come up and congratulate these fine young men who have earned Scouting's highest award, would you take a moment to look at the eagle that is on the Eagle Award? As you look closely you will notice the eagle that is on the Eagle Award is not a bald eagle. The eagle may have the white head and tail of the bald eagle, but it has the feathered legs and the wings of a golden eagle.

"Why has scouting chosen somewhat of a generic eagle to represent its highest award? The reason is that the bald eagle is exclusively a North American eagle, yet Scouting is a world-wide program. These fine young men are stepping into a brotherhood. A brotherhood of not just some of the finest young men this country has to offer, but a brotherhood of some of the finest young men worldwide.

"So yes, this is a very important evening, and for our new Eagle Scouts here this evening, patience. As many of the gentlemen in the Eagle's nest and the gentlemen in the audience as well can testify to, the 'Bald' Eagle Award will come much later in life, you'll get there.

"I've been asked to speak about the qualities of an eagle. An eagle has over seven thousand feathers. There are many Native Americans that believe when you say your prayers with an eagle feather, the eagle feather will carry your prayers to God. My eagle has over seven-thousand feathers, so I am in really good shape. All seven-thousand feathers weigh approximately twenty ounces in weight, so they are very light.

"The bones of birds are hollow so his skeletal structure again is only about twenty ounces in weight. Yet there is a portion of my eagle's body that represents more than half of his total body weight; the two large chest muscles — the pectoral muscles — which are the motors that he uses to drive his six-foot wingspan that will allow eagles to fly where hawks and falcons cannot. Eagles have been spotted at altitudes greater than thirty thousand feet. My eagle can comfortably soar in a forty-mile-an-hour wind that would ground a hawk or a falcon.

"My eagle has six hundred pounds per square inch of crushing power in his feet. He is capable of driving these four-inch long talons through my glove, crushing the bones in my hand. It's really good he likes me.

"Of course, the eyesight of an eagle is legendary. Let me tell you how well an eagle can see. With eyes larger than ours, the eagle can see approximately eight times further that we can, but you and I could get a pair of binoculars and we could see eight times further. The eagle also has six times the number of light sensitive cells (the rods and cones) in the back of the eye than we have, so everything that an eagle sees is six times clearer. My eagle can spot a jackrabbit five miles away.

"Tonight I'd like to make a few comparisons between my eagle 'Bud' and our new Eagle Scouts.

"The eagle and our Eagle Scouts, first, must have a clearness of vision: a clearness of vision to see opportunities in their lives. As the eagle and the Eagle Scout sit high upon the ledges surveying their domain with that clearness of vision; they are capable of seeing opportunities off in the future.

"The eagle has the largest brain. He is the most intelligent of all the birds of prey. Not only can the eagle and the Eagle Scout see opportunities in their lives, but they have the intelligence to recognize whether it is truly an opportunity or not.

"The eagle has infinite patience, which allows those opportunities to grow and to develop to their fullest potential. Then, and only then, does the eagle use his great physical strength to capitalize on those opportunities. That makes an eagle successful.

"An eagle is the world's greatest husband. Now, we have fine gentlemen in the Eagles Nest this evening, and fine gentlemen in the audience as well, and I would like you to think about this. Are you truly an eagle? For the male eagle returns to the nest site every spring on their anniversary, and the male eagle courts his lady eagle all over again as if it were their very first date.

"Gentlemen, do you court your wives? For an eagle does; the male eagle soars high over the ledges and dives recklessly down the face of cliffs to show off. The male eagle brings his lady eagle gifts: dead animals, sticks. Hey, it works for him.

"The eagle is the most loving and gentle of all fathers. When a young eaglet such as this one is hatched (or in the case of our young Scouts here today, were born), an eaglet is truly an infant. This eaglet weighing just a few ounces could barely hold up his head and could not focus those majestic and powerful eyes.

"As our young eaglets grow they watch the adult eagles. They learn how to use their feet, their wings; how to soar and what they can and cannot catch. At the appropriate time in our young eagles' lives, the adult eagle will kick the young eagles out of the nest and say, 'Now you're on your own.' With their new found independence and freedom, our young eagles now have the opportunity to spread their wings and soar.

"An eagle first must have a clearness of vision. An eagle is intelligent. An eagle has infinite patience. An eagle is the world's greatest husband and the most loving and gentle of all fathers. There is one more thing that an eagle is."

As I look toward our young Eagle Scouts, "There is only one way that you young men can become Eagles. You see, a hawk cannot raise an eagle, and a falcon cannot raise an eagle. Beautiful, powerful, wonderful creatures that they are, they cannot raise an eagle. The only way you young gentlemen tonight can become eagles, is that you must have been raised by eagles.

"The Eagle Scout award this evening is a testament to very fine parents, very fine grandparents, very fine church leaders, scout leaders, teachers and friends. The Eagle Award this evening is a testament to a very fine community, and if you young men will take upon yourselves the qualities of the eagle, you will not have to wear a badge on your shirt that says, 'I am an Eagle.' As you live these qualities everyone will know that you are truly an Eagle."

Bud is returned to his kennel and the Court of Honor is continued. The boys receive their Eagle Awards followed by the closing prayer and retiring of the colors. The Court of Honor is over.

Now the real work begins. I remove Bud from his kennel so that we may visit with everyone, to answer questions and to take photographs. Hundreds of people make for a very long evening. Bud is very patient but he lets me know when he is tired. When he jumps to his kennel, it's time to go home.

A Promise is a Promise

A few days after this particular Court of Honor, the mother of one of the young Eagle Scouts came into my pet shop and asked if she could speak with me for a moment. The look on her face reflected a deep sadness, and I asked, "What's wrong?"

She asked if I remembered a slender, elderly, white-haired gentleman that stood near Bud and me all evening? I replied, "Yes, I believe he stood off to my left side, but I don't remember him asking any questions."

The mother replied, "That was my father, and on the flight back to Salt Lake City after the Court of Honor, he passed away in the small airplane that my brother was flying."

Of course my response was, "I'm so very sorry".

Then she said, "I need to tell you something. My father was a retired airline pilot and his favorite things in the world were flying and eagles. For the last many years his health has been poor and he suffered a lot of pain and depression, which meant he could no longer fly.

"Having the opportunity to come and see his grandson receive his Eagle Award and to stand so close to you with your eagle, Bud, made my father's last evening very special. His last words before he passed away were how proud he was of his grandson and how truly amazing your eagle was. I just wanted to thank you for making my father's last moments on earth some of the best in his life."

We both were overcome with deep and powerful emotions, trying to hold back tears. She turned for the door, leaving me with a multitude of emotions, terribly sad, yet tremendously honored that I was able in some small way to help this gentleman's transition to the other side and to give comfort to the family.

I know that this is a long way around to make a point, but as I said before, I've always believed that we have come to earth with a mission in life. I've always believed in a pre-existence, a God, a Father, a Great Spirit. I've always believed that we are children of nobility, that we have left the comforts of a heavenly existence to come to earth to learn, to teach, to experience, and to honor our promises and commitments. I believe we made promises to each other, to help one another through the trials, pains and hardships that can occur here on earth.

Though we may have no memories of our previous life, we frequently will receive small promptings, a gentle guidance that will help steer us in the direction that our lives are meant to go. Often these promptings are no more than a childhood fantasy or a gentle heart's desire that seems to reoccur.

Not Just Another Court of Honor

One Saturday morning in late September I needed to hurry. There were lots of injured critters to care for before Bud and I could take off for the day. We had a long drive ahead of us, over four hundred miles round trip, to another Boy Scout Eagle Court of Honor.

I loaded a large airport kennel into the car and grabbed Bud's breakfast (a large dead rat). As I walked out to his house, Bud called to me, a beautiful, soft, airy whistle.

As I opened the door he ruffled up his feathers, which made him look more than twice as big. He smoothed his feathers back into place, stretched his long powerful wings, then with a single wingbeat flew the sixteen feet across his mews, landing on my glove and then began to feed.

He is neither gentle nor polite when he eats. His beak is designed to rip large chunks of flesh, and the rat was consumed in less than a minute. He ruffled up his feathers again as if to say, "Now I'm ready to go."

We left his mews and headed for the car where he jumped into his kennel. I closed the back of the car and we were off, heading north on I-15 to Provo, Utah. This is a drive that Bud and I have made hundreds of times before, providing wildlife programs throughout the state.

The time passed quickly and we arrived at the small community park where the Eagle Court of Honor was to be held. As we pulled into the parking lot, I noticed a large gathering of people around one of the park pavilions. I headed in that direction in hopes of meeting the family of the young man who had earned his eagle award.

You can always tell the mother of an Eagle Scout. She is the one that is frantically looking after every detail, a non-stop, polite whirlwind making sure that everything is done.

As I walked up to the mother of our Eagle Scout I introduced myself, "Hello, I am Martin Tyner, the eagle man."

I could see in her eyes a small sense of relief that the eagle had arrived, one less thing for her to worry about.

She asked, "Mr. Tyner can I help you with your eagle?"

I said, "Thank you but no, I am quite used to carrying him by myself."

Then she asked, "Do you mind if I walk with you? I would like to speak with you for a moment."

As we walked toward the parking lot and the car, the mother of our Eagle Scout seemed a little nervous and concerned. She said, "My son is an Eagle Scout and my son also has Down Syndrome. I wanted you to know that even with Down Syndrome my son earned his Eagle Award. He earned every merit badge, filled out all of his own paperwork, organized his eagle project and this year he will graduate from High School."

At this moment we had arrived at the car. I opened up the back and as I pulled the large kennel from the car, I told the mother, "I have no doubt that your son has earned his Eagle Award and that you are the Mother of an Eagle Scout."

A gentle smile came over her face as we walked back to the pavilion. I placed the large kennel on a table as people continued to gather.

I was introduced to our young Eagle Scout. Yes, he had Down Syndrome, but he also had a personality as large as the Wasatch Mountains. He had a joy and enthusiasm for life. He not only shook my hand but gave me a big hug, and with a great deal of enthusiasm thanked me for coming.

Back in the parking lot an ambulance had just arrived, followed by a second, and a third. I wondered what horrible event had just occurred to bring so many ambulances to this small community park. Behind the ambulances, a large number of eighteen-passenger vans pulled up. The parking lot was filling up quickly.

Then I witnessed one of the most unusual sights that I have ever seen. The doors of the ambulances were opened and gurneys were being pulled out; not empty gurneys, but gurneys with patients on them. They started to wheel the gurneys toward the pavilion where the Court of Honor ceremony was to be held. Following closely behind were dozens and dozens of senior citizens: some were in wheelchairs, some with walkers, and others with canes. They all were being assisted by health care workers.

As everyone arrived at the pavilion I found myself off to one side and a little bit lost in the crowd. The Court of Honor was called to order. A flag ceremony was provided by the local Boy Scout troop and an opening prayer was given. The Scout Master conducted the program.

The parents were asked to come up to the front and talk about their son. They spoke of the day he was born and the challenges he faced as a Down Syndrome baby. They spoke of an inner strength and determination that even when they believed something was impossible, their son had the strength and determination to carry on.

When the parents finished their talk, a gentleman in a white lab coat stepped up to the front. He was the director of a large assisted living home where all of the senior citizens who were in attendance that day had come from. He said, "Our young Eagle Scout came into my office one day and asked if he could give service to our assisted living home as his Eagle project.

"His Eagle project consisted of scrubbing floors, washing walls, emptying bedpans, doing whatever was needed for a period of six months. Not only did he complete his Eagle Scout project, but for the last two years he has continued to come every day after school, providing service to our residents and staff.

"The maintenance he performed was greatly appreciated, but the greatest gift of all was the love and friendship that he offered our residents. I would find him sitting for hours listening as some of our loneliest residents would share their life stories with him.

"This is why when the residents and staff of the home found out that Scotty was receiving his Eagle Award, everyone wanted to attend. As you can see, several of our residents are bedridden and the only way that they could attend Scotty's Court of Honor was to be transported by ambulances, which were generously donated for this event."

The audience broke out in applause, and when the applause settled down I was introduced. I walked up to the front, brought Bud out of his kennel and started my eagle talk. As I finished the talk and put Bud back in his kennel, it was time for the Eagle Award to be presented.

Our young Eagle Scout escorted his mother and father to the front. His mother pinned the Eagle Award on his uniform. It is customary that the Eagle Scout give his mother the appropriate Scout Salute, which is a big hug and a kiss on the cheek.

As tears rolled down his mother's face, his father stepped forward and removed the Boy Scout neckerchief and replaced it with an Eagle Scout neckerchief and an Eagle neckerchief slide. Our new young Eagle Scout gave his father a big hug as tears streamed down his father's face.

They were tears of joy and tears of pride, for a great young man, who is a true Eagle Scout.

Part Seven: Falconry & Wildlife Rehabilitation

Horrible the Falcon

"Horrible" was truly horrible!

Horrible was a large, female prairie falcon. The prairie falcon is one of the most aggressive, violent and difficult of all the large falcons. Most falconers would prefer to have a peregrine falcon or a gyr falcon because of their calm and gentle nature, but for some reason I've always been drawn to the prairie falcon, *Falco Mexicanis* (The Mexican falcon). Although most falconers would agree that a more suitable name would be *Falco Horibellis* (The Horrible Falcon).

Horrible took her violent and aggressive temperament to a new level. As she sat comfortably on my glove, she would look me square in the eye and scream at the top of her lungs. The only way I could get her to eat was to lightly pinch her toes, so she would think the food on my glove was biting her and then she would aggressively bite it back. This twenty-six ounce falcon was so aggressive that while hunting she knocked a nine-pound golden eagle out of the sky, unconscious. She killed a red-tailed hawk that was close to twice her size and strength. If there was a bird anywhere in the valley, she would attack it violently and drive it off, for this twenty-five mile stretch of desert belonged to her.

It was now time to return Horrible to the wild. This process is called hacking. Hacking allows us to gently introduce the bird to its natural environment, while at the same time breaking the bond between falconer and falcon. The process takes approximately three to four weeks and by this time the falcon no longer sees the falconer as a source of food, but just another human being to be avoided. To be completely honest, I was so glad when Horrible, the falcon, was finally gone.

The next spring a young male prairie falcon came into our rescue center. We called him Willie. He was a beautiful, small male with an unusually calm and gentle disposition (for a prairie falcon). I began the process to raise and train this young falcon, so that one day he could be returned to the wild.

Falconry techniques are by far the best process to raise and train young raptors and prepare them to be returned to the wild. Unfortunately, it is extremely time consuming and we are not able to offer this training to all of the raptors that enter our rescue facility. However, young Willie was a good candidate for the program.

First, the falcon must be full grown. In falconry terminology this is called "hard pinned," which is approximately nine weeks of age. Next, I must teach the bird to fly.

I place the young falcon on a low perch about a foot off the ground. Then I place the falcon's lure, which can best be described as a leather pigeon (a leather bag with leather wings), on the ground in front of the perch with a small portion of food tied to the lure by leather straps.

The young falcon will quickly learn to jump off the perch onto the lure and feed on the food provided. When the small meal is gone, I reach down with a gloved hand holding the rest of his dinner. The falcon then steps from the lure onto the glove for the rest of his meal.

The next day I repeat the process, moving the lure a little further from the perch. Soon the lure is placed on the ground twenty feet away as the young falcon eagerly flies the distance to obtain his reward.

The next step is to raise the lure slightly off the ground so the falcon must grab the lure in the air and take it to the ground to receive its reward. Again, the falcon steps off the lure and onto the glove for the rest of its dinner.

Next, I start gently swinging the lure so the falcon must catch a moving target. By this time the falcon is easily flying fifty feet to the lure. As the falcon becomes more enthusiastic with the game that we are playing, I continue to swing the lure harder and faster making it more difficult for the young falcon to catch the lure on his first pass.

When the lure is missed on the first pass, the falcon will pitch up into the sky, looking back for it. I immediately drop the lure to the ground as the falcon dives vertically, grabbing it with great enthusiasm and aggression, not wanting to miss it a second time. This is called "a stoop to the lure."

I slowly increase the number of stoops to the lure from one, to two, to five, to ten, to as many as fifty. Each time the falcon misses the lure, he becomes increasingly motivated to catch the lure on the next pass. This builds up the falcon's physical strength, his agility and his ability to catch fast-moving objects.

Susan Tyner

Until this point in time, I have been exercising the falcon in an area dedicated to lure flying: an open field free of obstructions, such as tall brush, fences and power lines. Once the young falcon becomes physically fit, strong and fast, it is then time to teach the falcon to gain altitude.

A falcon does not have the physical strength that a large hawk or eagle has, capable of binding to large quarry with its feet and killing it on the ground. A falcon relies on a high-speed, vertical dive, reaching speeds up to two hundred miles an hour, striking its quarry dead with its feet. For a large falcon to be truly successful, it must learn how to fly high and dive vertically with pinpoint accuracy.

You might wonder how an earthbound creature like humans can teach a falcon to soar high in the sky. I have always let Mother Nature teach this lesson for me.

I take the falcon out to the desert where there are miles of open sky. I release the falcon to the sky as he looks forward to the game of catching the lure. The falcon circles about one hundred feet over my head. I do not bring out the lure. As the young falcon begins to get bored, he'll make low and fast passes trying to encourage me to bring out his toy, but the lure will not come. He becomes bored and frustrated and will drift away looking for something to do.

At this time I hope the falcon will find a column of warm, rising air, called a thermal. When a young falcon finds his first thermal it is almost like a child who first learns to ride a bicycle. You can see the joy and excitement as the falcon fans his tail, extends his wings, and allows this column of warm, rising air to take him skyward.

When the falcon reaches significant altitude (five hundred to one thousand feet), it is time to coax him back overhead. I pull the lure from the vest, wave it to the falcon to get his attention and then hide it back in the vest.

If everything has gone well, the falcon will drift back overhead to see if I am ready to bring out his toy, but instead of producing the lure, a live pigeon is released.

Please understand that in order for the falcon to be returned to the wild successfully, he must know how to hunt. Like so many people that raise chickens, sheep and cows for food, we must raise pigeons, not only to feed the injured wildlife that we care for, but to teach some of the younger birds how to hunt successfully.

As the pigeon flutters away, the falcon's instinct kicks in and he will dive vertically reaching speeds close to two hundred miles an hour, striking the pigeon with his feet, killing it instantly. As the pigeon tumbles to the earth the falcon will circle around, land on the pigeon and begin to feed.

Soon the falcon will have the opportunity to fly against some of our best, high performance, racing pigeons that it will have little or no chance of catching. This continues to build his strength, his endurance and his accuracy as an avian hunter, bringing him closer to the day when he will return to the wild as a successful master of the sky.

Now that I had completed the lure training, it was time to introduce my young falcon, Willie, to thermals. It was early fall on a beautiful, warm afternoon as we headed out to the open desert. Once we arrived at my favorite flying field, I unhooded Willie and released him to the sky.

As was expected, Willie circled over my head at about a hundred feet waiting for me to bring out his lure. Suddenly, directly above us, two thousand feet plus, a large female falcon appeared. She had just rolled over and started her death stoop! She was going to kill my new little falcon!

I quickly reached into the back pocket of my hunting vest, pulled out the lure and threw it to the ground. As Willie came to the lure, I immediately dove over the top of him, just as the large, female falcon tried to fly through me to kill him. She deflected off my back, landed ten feet away, looked me square in the eye and screamed at the top of her lungs. It was horrible, and yes, it was Horrible!

Horrible recognized my truck. For the next three years, every time I went out on the desert to exercise my falconry birds, I would have to take a sacrificial pigeon for the falcon goddess.

Luckily Horrible has moved to the next valley over and for the last several years she has been raising "Little Horribles," and yes, she is a wonderful mother.

Tough Little Owl

It was ten o'clock at night when two teenage boys were driving westbound on Highway 14 about three miles from town. They saw a quick movement in the headlights and heard a thump on the windshield. They stopped their car and backed up to see what they had hit. Lying in the middle of the road was a small grey owl, a screech owl. They picked up the dead owl, placed it in a plastic grocery bag, dropped it in the trunk of their car and went home for the night.

The next morning they arrived at my pet shop with the plastic bag in hand. "Mr. Tyner," one of the boys said, "We were driving down Highway 14 last night and accidently hit a small owl. We did not know what to do with it so we brought it to you."

As they handed me the bag with the dead owl, I told the boys, "Go ahead and take off, I'll take care of it." Everyone in town knows when they come across an injured critter, especially birds of prey that I am the guy to bring it to.

After the boys left I opened the plastic bag and looked inside. To my surprise and horror, the owl took a breath. "Oh, my gosh!" I thought, "This poor thing. I can't believe he's still alive."

The right side of his face looked crushed and deformed, covered in mud and blood. I knew that there was no way that he was going to survive. I also knew that I was probably going to have to put him to sleep.

Even after being a wildlife rehabilitator for so many years, it still takes a little bit of courage to put one of these beautiful, little creatures to sleep. So I placed him in a small, plastic pet carrier, set it on the shelf in the back room and continued doing my chores. After about an hour my conscience got the better of me. I could not just let that poor little creature suffer. As much as I hated this part of the job, I knew I was going to have to put him to sleep.

So, I mustered up my courage, walked into the back room and removed the small pet carrier from the shelf. As I looked inside the container, the little owl was standing. "Oh my gosh, you poor thing," I whispered, "Let me see what I can do."

For some of my most critically ill patients I mix up a special diet containing Pedialite®, which adds fluids and electrolytes, Nutri-Cal, a high calorie concentrated protein and vitamin supplement, and ground mice.

Steve Allred

A quick word to the wise: if any of you happen to stop by my home you probably don't want to use the blender.

After removing the needle from a large syringe and replacing it with a small soft rubber tube, I filled the syringe with the liquid diet. I gently opened the little owl's mouth, slid the small, soft, rubber tube down its throat and administered a small portion of food. I placed the owl back in the carrier and went back to work. I returned a couple of hours later and the owl was looking a little better, so I repeated the process.

After a couple of days of around-the-clock intensive care, the little owl had made a remarkable recovery, with the exception of the right side of his face and his right eye. It was now time to take him to my veterinarian and deal with the head injuries. I didn't want to open the eye without being at the vet's office in a surgical situation, so if there was excessive bleeding, we could deal with the problem.

When we arrived at the vet's office, we moved the little owl immediately into surgery where we gently and carefully cleaned the right side of his face and prepared to open the eye. As serious as the injury looked, I fully expected to find the eye blown out, but to my surprise the eye was still there. The cornea was dented in and the eye was full of blood. Obviously, he was blind in his right eye and could never be returned to the wild.

At this moment, I had a difficult decision to make. As a federally licensed wildlife rehabilitator, I only have three options. First, return everything that I possibly can back to the wild. Second, if the animal is non-releasable but otherwise healthy, place it in a federally licensed educational program. The third option is euthanasia.

Acknowledging the fact that this little owl had fought courageously to survive, I made the decision to see if he could withstand the stress of captivity. Imagine being a small, delicate, wild owl and having to sit quietly on a glove in an auditorium with five hundred noisy children. That's asking a great deal of any animal, let alone a wild one.

I placed the little screech owl in one of our smaller flight facilities where he was allowed to recuperate and exercise. After approximately three months of recuperation, it was time to remove the little owl from our rehabilitation permits and transfer him to our educational permits; to outfit him with small leather anklets and small leather straps called jesses, preparing him for the gentling process called manning.

As I walked into the flight facility to gather up the little owl, I noticed that his right eye had regained its normal shape. The blood had receded out of the eye and the eye looked wonderful.

We did a series of flight tests covering the owl's left eye, and he was able to navigate around the flight facility using only his right eye. He was even able to fly down to the holding container where we would place live mice for him to catch.

We picked up the screech owl, took him back to the mountains and released him to the wild where he belonged. From dead in a plastic bag, to released back into the wild. That was one tough little owl!

Vampire Bat

I'm on call twenty-four hours a day, seven days a week to rescue the sick, injured and orphaned wildlife of Southern Utah.

The telephone rang at two o'clock in the morning! It was police dispatch. "Mr. Tyner, I'm sorry to wake you, but you need to come into town. There is a vampire bat flying around inside someone's home."

"It's two o'clock in the morning. I'm sorry, I'm not in the mood for this," I told police dispatch. "We are not in Transylvania nor are we in South America. There are no vampire bats in Utah."

The dispatcher insisted that this was not a joke. The officer indicated that this was the largest bat that he had ever seen and that I needed to come into town. So I rolled out of bed, got dressed, jumped in the car, and headed for town.

I couldn't imagine what this was. I've gotten some strange phone calls in my time and have driven hundreds of miles to rescue an eagle walking on the ground that ended up to be a neighbor's chicken. I've been called out by an elderly woman who reportedly had a giant snake in her back yard. It was nothing more than a corn stalk from her garden. There was a cougar that ended up being a neighbor's big, yellow Labrador retriever. I think you get the point.

As I arrived at the home where the vampire bat had been reported, I found six police cars surrounding the house. It must have been a slow night. As I walked in the front door, I found two officers in the living room hiding behind the couch with their pistols drawn. As a small, aerial creature flew by, I reach up and grabbed it with my bare hand, much to the horror of the officers.

As I got control of the little creature I said, "It's a pygmy owl! They're completely harmless. Isn't it cute?"

The pygmy owl is a beautiful, little owl, only about five inches tall.

Susan Tyner

As the officers came out from behind the couch, I gave them a quick lesson on bird and bat identification. I placed the owl in a small travel container and headed for home. After a thorough health inspection and a good meal, the little owl was returned to the wild.

The officers here in Southern Utah are some of the most noble and courageous gentlemen I have ever met and I have the utmost respect for them. They are just terrified of bats.

Bud's Last Hunt

September sixth, it was a beautiful, early, fall morning. Blue skies, no breeze, it was going to be a great day for Bud and I to go out chasing jackrabbits.

As I walked toward Bud's house I could hear the bells attached to his anklets as he bounced around with great anticipation for the morning hunt. I stepped into his mews as he ruffled up his feathers. He stretched his wings and jumped to my glove as if to say, "Let's go."

107

We walked across the yard and into the carport as Bud jumped to his scale. Five pounds, twelve ounces, he was at the perfect weight. He jumped back to my glove. As I opened the back of the car he eagerly jumped into his large airport kennel, turned around and waited for me to close the door so that we could be on our way. I did a quick check of his equipment and with a pocket full of tidbits (dead mice), we were ready to head out toward the lava flow. It was our favorite place to hunt.

I parked the car off the side of the dirt road, and I could hear the leg bells ringing. Bud could hardly wait for his opportunity to fly free. I removed him from his kennel and placed a small transmitter on his leg so that if he happened to catch a rabbit four or five miles away I could find him.

Bud soared off my glove and headed directly for the lava flow. Working along the ridge, he landed on a large boulder about half way up the hill. He looked back in my direction, and I knew that was my signal to get busy. I headed out west across the desert with my flushing stick in hand beating the brush in the hopes of flushing a rabbit for him soon.

I heard the bells behind me. I turned and looked back to see Bud had taken flight. He was heading north along the ridge gaining more altitude. He then turned south searching for any kind of lift that he could find to help carry him skyward.

As Bud climbed higher in the sky, a large, female golden eagle appeared over the ridge from the east and began to soar along the ridge with Bud. The sight of watching these two magnificent golden eagles soaring together was an amazing sight.

Suddenly Bud set his wings, pulled them in tight against his body and started to drop from the sky in a high-speed, shallow dive. About a half-mile behind me there was a rabbit traveling through the heavy brush.

Bud pulled up vertically, looked over his right shoulder trying to spot the rabbit below, then folded up tight and fell vertically into the heavy brush. Before I could get to him, he was back in the sky

Noella Ballenger

heading for the lava flow again.

This was a common sight. Bud's success ratio was that he would catch one rabbit for every forty rabbits I flushed. This was average for most golden eagles.

Bud returned to the lava flow and worked his way up the ridge. He looked back at me again as I headed off through the brush trying to flush rabbits.

After a couple of hours of beating the brush and flushing rabbits it was time to go home. Though we may not have caught any rabbits today, we had a great deal of fun and exercise. I loaded Bud back up in the car and we headed for home.

After we arrived home Bud stepped out of the kennel onto my glove. Then I carried him out to the weathering yard where he could relax and bathe and enjoy the day as I headed for work.

At five o'clock in the evening I headed out to the weathering yard to pick up Bud and to put him to bed for the night. As I approached the weathering yard Bud was sitting quietly on his perch. I put my gloved hand down for him to step up onto and something just didn't seem right as he stepped onto my glove.

He wasn't steady. He wasn't solid. Bud just didn't feel right on the glove. Something was desperately wrong.

I gave Bud a thorough physical inspection, there were no injuries. There was nothing in the weathering yard that could have harmed him.

My mind quickly raced through all of the illnesses and injuries that could have caused Bud to feel weak and unsteady and the most horrible thought came to mind. "It can't be! No, it can't be West Nile Virus!"

West Nile Virus had been reported in eastern Utah but there were no signs of West Nile Virus in Southwestern Utah, or at least not yet.

West Nile Virus is transferred by mosquitoes. It started on the east coast and as it moved west it devastated bird of prey populations. One state might lose Cooper's hawks, another might lose great horned owls, while another might lose crows. West Nile Virus had proven to be one hundred percent fatal in adult golden eagles.

It can't be West Nile!

I brought Bud into the house and placed him on a perch in the basement. I immediately started him on the treatment for West Nile.

West Nile is a virus and the only thing that you can do is treat the symptoms. Anti-inflammatory drugs, subcutaneous IVs, a liquid diet, and do our best to keep him warm, quiet and comfortable.

I spent three days sitting on the basement floor as Bud slowly lost control of his body. West Nile causes the brain to swell. It is a cruel and painful death. The only thing that brought Bud any comfort was for him to lie in my lap, to feel my touch and to hear my voice.

In all my years as a wildlife rehabilitator I have rescued hundreds of eagles and returned them to the wild, but I couldn't save Bud. This was the first time in my life that I ever heard an eagle cry.

Bud passed away Friday evening, September 9, 2005.

Farewell Bud! We Will Miss You! *by Susan Tyner*

Bud, the golden eagle usually seen with his human companion, Martin Tyner, has left this earthly world to soar among the angels forever. The West Nile Virus has finally made its way to Southern Utah, including locations where Bud has lived and hunted for the past fifteen years. The first symptoms of slight tremors and weakness hit Bud suddenly on Tuesday evening, September 6. Although treatment began immediately to try to save him, he lost his battle Friday evening September 9, 2005.

Bud, who died at the age of sixteen years, has been a member of our community for the past fifteen years. His story is unique and he has touched the lives and hearts of hundreds of thousands of people in his fifteen years of service.

Bud was the first eagle in the United States to be legally trapped for the purpose of falconry and educational programs. He was considered depredation (a threat to livestock) and was trapped with permits issued to Martin Tyner through the U.S. Fish and Wildlife Service, the U.S. Department of Agriculture, and the Utah Division of Wildlife Resources. Bud was approximately one year of age.

After this sudden change in his life, Bud soon came to trust his new human companion. There developed a rare and unique relationship between man and eagle, which could easily been seen by just observing the two of them together.

111

Bud has provided service to not only to our community, Cedar City, but has also been the highlight of educational programs provided regularly throughout all of Utah and Clark County, Nevada. He has traveled as far as Phoenix, Arizona; Roswell, New Mexico; El Paso, Texas; and most recently, Coeur d' Alene, Idaho; and Augusta, Montana.

Steve Allred

Bud was the highlight of the Utah Shakespearean Festival, Green Show, for many years. He assisted in a class taught by Martin Tyner on *"The Art and Craft of Medieval Falconry"* at Southern Utah University. He has participated in Cedar City's annual Midsummer Renaissance Faire for the last fifteen years. Just last winter, Bud was an invited guest of the State of Utah, House of Representatives, where he joined Martin Tyner in receiving a citation for their unselfish educational service pertaining to birds of prey indigenous to the State of Utah.

Bud has become not only a teacher, a symbol and mascot, but an ambassador for the Southwest Wildlife Foundation, a non-profit organization created to provide wildlife rescue and rehabilitation to Utah's native species wildlife and provide wildlife educational programs to the schools, scouts and other organizations. He has appeared at hundreds of schools, giving thousands of children the opportunity to see a live eagle close up, helping to teach a greater appreciation for our native wildlife and environment.

Bud has appeared at hundreds of Boy Scout Eagle Courts of Honor where he and Martin compare the superb qualities of an eagle with that of the Eagle Scout, commending the Eagle Scout for his accomplishments and challenging him to live up to a life time of high standards. They have also challenged and inspired many young boys of scouting age to set high goals, including achieving the rank of Eagle Scout.

Bud convinced the new owners of Utah Power, Pacificorp (now Rocky Mountain Power) a few years ago, to donate 22.6 beautiful acres of canyon property on Highway 14 in Cedar City, to the Southwest Wildlife Foundation for the purpose of building a world class wildlife rescue facility and nature park.

He inspired a gift of $25,000 from Fred Lampropolous, CEO of Merit Medical Systems, towards this facility. Although Bud is no longer on the earth with us, I am sure he will inspire those that can help to reach our goal of $300,000 for the first phase of this facility to begin construction.

In fifteen years, Bud has provided educational programs to more than 300,000 people with the greatest impact and focus on children and scouts. In his last few years he has participated in over a hundred programs a year, reaching well over 20,000 people annually.

He has given his complete love and trust to his best friend and companion, Martin Tyner for fifteen years and he has given the most noble service, teaching, and inspiration, to thousands.

"BUD, YOU HAVE BECOME A MEMBER OF OUR FAMILY, AND OUR COMMUNITY. YOU HAVE TOUCHED OUR LIVES AND HEARTS. WE WILL MISS YOU DEARLY."

A New Friend

I had grieved deeply for Bud for months, sinking into depression and avoiding people as much as possible. Finally, seven months after Bud's passing, in mid-April the phone rang. It was the U.S. Fish and Wildlife Service out of Denver, Colorado. A rancher was complaining that an eagle was a threat to his livestock. They needed someone to travel to Wyoming to rescue the eagle before it got shot.

I met with Sam Crowe of the U.S. Department of Agriculture just outside of Lyman, Wyoming. He guided us out to the depredation area where we set up a bait station to trap the offending eagle.

It took about a week to get the eagle to come to the bait station where it could be caught and removed from the depredation area. This was a large, male, golden eagle or maybe a small female. It was certainly larger, stronger and more powerful than Bud.

As Susan and I were heading home, there was a sense of excitement. We had a new eagle for our school and scout programs: a new eagle for my falconry, and hopefully, a new friend.

As we arrived home, I took the hooded eagle down to the basement where it was dark and cool to begin our falconry wake. It became obvious very quickly, "This was not Bud!"

This eagle was not only bigger and stronger than Bud, but it was far more aggressive and dangerous. I was going to have to be extremely careful. This eagle wanted to hurt me, to bite my face and crush my arm. With a calm voice and a gentle hand I was slowly able to gain his trust and confidence.

Susan asked me frequently, "What are you going to name the new eagle?"

The truth was I had no idea. I certainly did not want to call him Bud two.

Susan suggested that we let the community name the eagle. "How about a 'name the eagle' contest?"

Susan Tyner

Name for an Eagle

The response to our name the eagle contest had been amazing. We've received somewhere in the neighborhood of three hundred suggestions, many with personal stories, names of people that have touched their lives, and many descriptive names of what an eagle is.

As I sat down and reviewed the suggestions, it gave me a wonderful opportunity to look back on the life and service of my previous golden eagle, Bud. In the nearly sixteen years that we were together, we traveled through much of the western United States providing wildlife programs for schools and scouts and community events.

One of the most important programs was the Eagle Scout Court of Honor, for which we participated in hundreds. What a marvelous opportunity it was to travel around this country and stand before groups of young scouts with Bud on my glove and encourage these boys to become Eagles.

As I looked back on the relationship that Bud and I had, some amazing attributes started to come to mind. As I thought about Bud, for some reason trustworthy came to mind, for Bud was incredibly loyal. He was so helpful in getting our message out, he was my best friend. And for just a moment, I remembered my days as a tenderfoot scout and standing before an auditorium full of people, reciting the scout laws. *"A scout is trustworthy, loyal, helpful, friendly, courteous, kind, obedient, cheerful, thrifty, brave, clean, and reverent."*

All of a sudden I realized that after so many years of encouraging young scouts to become Eagles, my eagle, Bud, had truly become a scout. The name that I was looking for, for our new eagle, was a name that would reflect not what the eagle is, but what the eagle would hopefully become. So the name we chose for my new best friend was "Scout".

This was one of the first names suggested and also one of the last names suggested, and of course my wife, Susan, came up with the best line, "We may not be sure if the eagle is a Boy Scout or a Girl Scout, but it is definitely an Eagle Scout!"

Scout and I are looking forward to hitting the road and providing wildlife programs for many years to come.

Non-Survivor

Please don't let the title throw you. No one could have guessed that this young golden eagle, who was not supposed to survive, would come to touch the lives and heal the hearts of so many.

Non-survivor's life started out like most young, golden eagles. Eighty percent of all birds of prey do not survive their first year in the wild. The wild is a tough place to make a living.

This young eagle began life with as good a chance as any. His nest was on a small butte approximately two-hundred feet above the desert floor. Eagle country! Sage brush bordered by pinion pine and juniper forest.

A small herd of wild mustangs frequently moved through the valley. Antelope fed below the nest site, and five miles to the south there were large alfalfa farms. This year looked to be a good year with large populations of prairie dogs and jackrabbits. The eagle pair should have no problem feeding their young.

Their nest was large and well constructed, approximately six feet across and fifteen feet deep. It was an old nest, belonging to a well-established pair of eagles. As winter gave way to early spring, activity around the nest increased. Mom and dad were eager to make necessary repairs from the winter's damage. New branches, sticks, twigs, and bark, were carefully layered; not only to reinforce the nest, but to add to its comfort for mama eagle and the chicks that would hatch a month and a half later.

Two eggs were laid, and with the protection and care of the parent eagles, both eggs hatched. Eaglets are beautiful – pure white, fluffy, delicate creatures. Seeing them in their fragile new-born condition, it is hard to imagine that they will one day be the large and powerful masters of the sky.

Eagle parents are remarkable, gentle creatures. They care for their young with tenderness and patience. As the sun rises high in the sky and the days become warm, mama eagle will spread her wings over the nest to shade her chicks from the heat, sacrificing her personal comfort for their well-being.

The young eaglets grow quickly. From the day they hatch until the time they are full grown and starting to fly is just a short twelve weeks. Throughout this growth period the chicks consume large quantities of food, mostly jackrabbits and prairie dogs, but the eagle is an opportunistic predator and will feed on road kill and other forms of carrion.

Soon, our young eagle was standing on the nest, exercising his six-foot wingspan. Feeling the desert breeze encouraged him to work hard, instinctively preparing his body for flight. Like most young eagles, the first flight would be more of an accident than a purposeful attempt to soar the skies.

Our young friend was on the edge of the nest flapping his wings, building his strength. A gust of wind came through and lifted him three feet above the nest. He glided forward and suddenly realized, "I'm flying!"

As awkward as a child taking his first steps, the young eagle was unsteady on his wings. As he glided to the bottom of the cliff, his landing was far from graceful.

Martin Tyner

Mom and dad returned with food. They fed the young eagle on the ground. With a strong sense of determination, he flapped his wings and jumped from rock to rock. He worked his way back up the cliff to the top where the lesson was learned. Now it was a matter of honing his skills and learning to use the air currents.

As the eagle's skills increased, he followed mom and dad further away from the safety of the cliffs, out over the open desert as the parents searched for their next meal. This was where the problem began.

On a beautiful, warm July morning, the young eagle was floating on the desert breeze watching mom and dad attempting to catch a jackrabbit near the alfalfa fields to the south. Suddenly he found himself in a column of warm rising air called a thermal. As he entered the thermal, the lift was wonderful. He soared effortlessly higher and higher. The lift became stronger: five hundred feet per minute, one thousand feet per minute, two thousand feet per minute.

Our young eagle did not have the strength or experience to handle the suck from a large cumulus cloud that was developing above him. Within minutes he was in the clouds with zero visibility. Rain and fierce turbulence tumbled the young eagle. It was a terrifying experience.

When the eagle broke free of the clouds, he was many miles away from his nest. Lost and disoriented, he glided into an unfamiliar valley. Without his parents to care for him, to feed him and to teach him to hunt, his chances for survival were poor. For days he wandered up and down the valley, calling for his parents. Each day without food he became weaker. No longer having the strength to fly and finding himself on the desert floor in temperatures that well exceeded one hundred degrees, his life was all but over.

I received a phone call from a family out recreating on ATVs. They reported with much concern that there was an eagle on the ground in the middle of the desert. It was unable to fly.

I threw a large airport kennel in the car. My wife and I started the forty-five minute drive to the location where the eagle was spotted. When we arrived we found the family sitting on their vehicles at a safe distance watching the young eagle as it struggled to stand on a small rise in the terrain.

I grabbed my pole net from the car and headed across the desert. I hoped that when the eagle saw me, he would fly away and be just fine. This was not the case. He could barely move. I scooped him up and gave him a quick visual inspection which told me how critical the situation was.

The eagle weighed less than half his normal body weight. He was horribly emaciated and dehydrated, but worst of all were his eyes. As a wildlife rehabilitator for nearly forty years, I've seen those eyes before. He was still breathing but his eyes were dead, lifeless, and dark.

We headed back to the car as quickly as possible knowing that he probably wouldn't survive the forty-five minute trip home. We immediately started him on fluids, but there was little or no chance for his survival.

We checked on his progress approximately every half hour. For the first several hours we expected to find him dead and have to bag and freeze him. By morning he was incredibly weak, but he could stand. We continued a liquid diet along with small pieces of jackrabbit that we pushed down his throat.

After a couple of days he was moving freely around the chamber, but what impressed me the most were his eyes. The fierceness, the strength, and the light were back in his eyes.

I picked him up to hand feed him again. "Ouch!" He reached over and bit a chunk of flesh out of my hand. What a great feeling, he was ready to fight for his life!

It wasn't long before he was feeding himself, tearing apart rabbit carcasses and exercising his wings in the flight facility. Now it was just a matter of time to let him regain his strength, make sure he understood how to kill jackrabbits, and give him as much exercise as possible. When he was ready we would return him to the sky, giving him a second chance at life.

Most of the time the story ends here, the young eagle is released in the hopes that he will live a long life, soaring the skies, hunting jackrabbits and prairie dogs, and one day finding a mate.

But this time things would be a little different.

As we prepared the young eagle for his return to the wild, a horrible tragedy occurred in Central Utah. A coal mine collapsed just outside of Huntington, Utah. Six miners were trapped two thousand feet below ground.

A heroic effort to save these miners turned into another tragedy when a second collapse killed three rescue miners and injured eight others.

The pain and grief of this tragedy was felt across the country. Every night we watched the news. Nothing good was happening for the families of the trapped miners.

Having the young eagle ready to go, I made an offer to the people of Huntington, and the families of the lost miners: an opportunity to release the eagle in honor of their loved ones.

Native people from around the world believe that if you say your prayers with an eagle feather, the eagle feather will carry your prayers to God. This young eagle has over seven thousand feathers, and after forty years of wildlife rescue and releasing many eagles back to the wild, I know how healing and powerful an eagle release is.

I once had an opportunity to sit down with a Paiute spiritual leader, and he told me the story of the eagle. He said the eagle was once human and the most noble and courageous of the native people. He was asked to come and sit in council in heaven. This noble brave told the Great Spirit, "I cannot sit in council in heaven because I cannot fly".

So the Great Spirit turned him into an eagle, and the eagle was given a calling: to remain on earth by night and collect all the prayers from the people of the nation, and by day to ride the columns of warm rising air, thermals (which is what got our young eagle in trouble in the first place), to heaven to deliver the prayers to the Great Spirit. Then to receive all of the blessings from the Great Spirit and bring them back to the people of the nation.

For this reason I made the offer of an eagle release to the people of Huntington and the families of the miners. After the offer was made reality set in, "What have I done?"

This eagle is as wild and unpredictable as any eagle I have ever cared for. What if he flew violently against the wall of his chamber and injured himself? What if he was bitten by a mosquito and died of West Nile Virus? How horrible it would be to call up the families of the lost miners to say, "I'm sorry I can not bring the eagle because he died." Tragedy on top of tragedy on top of tragedy! I lost several nights' sleep worrying about how this would go.

The day of the eagle release arrived. We caught the eagle out of the flight chamber, hooded him and placed him in an airport kennel for the trip. When we arrived in the town of Huntington, we met with Councilwoman Julie Jones and her husband. They led us up the canyon, past the Crandall Canyon Mine site, to the top of a mountain, to a road called Skyline Drive, part of the Great Western Trail.

What an amazing place! You could see for miles in every direction. I recognized that it was actually a major raptor migration path. We watched a variety of raptors soaring as we scouted out a suitable area for the release and waited for friends and families of the lost miners to join us.

We stood at the top of the mountain, on the edge of a cliff. A steep slope dropped down into a deep canyon which opened into a large valley below. The breeze was perfect, with light, fluffy clouds floating overhead.

As family and friends gathered there was a feeling of deep sadness and almost unbearable grief. I was introduced to the wife of one of the rescue miners. I was told by a family friend that her husband died while saving the lives of two other miners during the second mine collapse. Everyone knew him as "Bird".

Wendy Black, the wife of the fallen miner, had been chosen to do the release. I started to explain the process we would use in releasing the eagle, and she said she was terrified of birds, the only reason she would do it was to honor her husband.

Trying to set her mind at ease, I explained that I had been rescuing and releasing eagles for nearly forty years, and no one had ever gotten a scratch. As long as she followed my instructions, she would be just fine.

Nearly seventy family members came to the mountain top. As more and more arrived, I began to get nervous. A single thunder cell was building right overhead. I was worried about the potential of rain and lightning coming down at the top of the mountain.

At the appointed time, after everyone was there, Mayor Hilary Gordan spoke a few words to the group. Maggie McMullin read a poem that she had written a few days earlier. A prayer was given by a brother of one of the lost miners, and then it was time for the eagle release.

During the mayor's talk, the poem, and the prayer, it was cold and dark and a light rain started to fall. When it was time for the eagle release, the sun broke through the clouds, warmth returned to the top of the mountain, and I began my talk, the story of the eagle.

I removed the hooded eagle from his kennel and asked each of the nine families, before the eagle was released, if they would like to come forward and give a family prayer so the eagle could carry their prayers to God.

The first to come up was the grandfather of one of the lost miners. Frail and elderly, surrounded by family he placed his hand on the back of the hooded eagle and with tears of grief, prayed for his grandson. This process was repeated for all of the lost miners: some prayed out loud, some in silence, all with grief and pain.

Healer of Angels

The time came to release the eagle. I asked Wendy Black to step forward. I repeated my previous instructions on how to safely hold the eagle. I passed the bird into her arms, and when the eagle rested easily I removed the hood.

In a whispered voice, Wendy said, "This is for you, Sweetheart."

As the eagle was released he soared out over the canyon and then circled back over the families. He landed on the top of a hill behind us, where he spent a few minutes looking about, surveying the landscape.

He then soared from the top of the mountains, set his wings in the prevailing lift and rode the air currents straight up above us until he disappeared into the clouds carrying our prayers to the heavens.

Eagle *by Maggie Fugate McMullin*

The Healer of Angels has heard our cries.

He had brought to us the Eagle,

Messenger to the Heavens,

Eagle take our sorrows, our loneliness and fear,

Take to the skies lighten our hearts and souls.

Eagle we hoped, prayed, and believed,

Lost alone in fear of the unknown,

Fly above this mountain,

Take our grief and pain,

Ease this heavy burden we carry

Eagle we mourn for those we lost,

Those so precious and loved,

Taken so sudden in darkness and fear,

Those who were so brave who followed to save,

Taken too soon.

Eagle fly high and touch the heavens,

Fly to the stars take our sadness,

Take their precious spirits to soar above the skies,

Fly in the bright sun and clouds,

Soar with the angels,

Eagle take our lost ones,

Release them free to fly above,

Free to watch down upon us,

Free to move on,

Free to join those who have gone before.

Eagle bless us left behind,

Lift our spirits to the skies,

May we see you soar high,

Remind us of those we loved and lost,

Let us believe again live again.

Martin Tyner

Eagle soar to the heavens,

Dip through the clouds,

Help us see to the future,

Remember the past,

Cherish the present,

Eagle we are grateful,

Fly high and lead us,

Give us hope, peace and love,

Eagle stay in our dreams,

Healer of Angels our greatest thanks.

Dedicated to the Eagle and The Healer of Angels

Maggie Fugate McMullin 8/23/07

Part Eight: Back to the Hunt

In a steady cold wind on a late January afternoon, snow crunched underfoot as the old falconer climbed higher up the ridge of an ancient lava flow. He came here often to find his inner strength and peace. The sun shining in the sky gave little warmth that day, but there was warmth deep inside him that spread as he watched his golden eagle soaring effortlessly a few hundred yards away.

Suddenly, his attention was diverted by the sound of a cell phone. The old falconer reached deep into his pocket removing the phone.

"Hello, this is Martin.

"OK, are you sure it's an eagle?

"Minersville Highway, two hundred yards north of mile marker forty-six, east side of the road. I got it. I'm leaving right now; I'll be there in twenty minutes."

Martin heads down the back side of the ridge to his truck below. For a moment, Scout, the golden eagle, is confused but realizes quickly that their hunt together is being cut short. Just before Martin reaches the truck he blows his whistle and throws out a lure.

Scout lands on the lure, then quickly steps to the glove receiving a small portion of his meal as Martin says, "Sorry Scout, we've got to go. There is another injured eagle."

Scout turns and quickly jumps into his kennel. Martin closes the back of the truck and the two of them head off to rescue another critter.

Notes from Bud's Friends

"...I will always know Bud as something more than an eagle who I

happened to see a couple of times around town. I saw him enough,

I think, to feel a special kinship and understand a side of him few were blessed to see. He still soars in my heart.

"I will never forget looking into his eyes and wondering what he thought of this stupid human who stood there, jaw agape, pondering his splendor. He was, perhaps, the most beautiful creature among nature's many beautiful creatures. He had strength, tranquility and, I think, a sense of humor. He also had a sense of place. He knew who he was and what he was. His picture hangs on my wall. I selfishly thought of him like I do my own animal companions and am deeply saddened.

"I also know that he is soaring again in that special place God saves for the creatures who comfort us in this world. I cannot imagine that his journey has ended. It is, I truly believe, only beginning. He joins a couple of friends of mine who I, too, have lost over the years who left indelible marks on my soul.

"I will be eternally grateful for you allowing me to meet him and become so close to him.

"Bless you both at this time. I know how it feels, I truly do, and my heart goes to you both. Ed"

"One of the most memorable times of my life involved meeting Martin and being introduced to the wonders of Parowan Gap. It

was an experience so powerful it brought tears to my eyes. Visiting the Gap was not the only sacred experience I was to have that day. Before we left, Martin opened the back of his van and introduced me to the mysterious creature that I had heard but not yet seen as we drove around that day. I didn't know what to expect. Martin told me "Bud" was the source of the noise, but I didn't know what Bud was. When I saw Bud, I was captivated. I can hardly articulate the emotion that moment inspired. It was awe-inspiring and humbling. One of THE most profound moments of my life.

Thank you, Martin. And THANK YOU, BUD! You have given me an exceptional gift. With honor, respect, and gratitude, Joy"

"...I remember the first time we saw an Eagle presentation with Martin and our son Trued, who was able to have a picture when he promised to become an Eagle Scout. He was 8 then. At age 13 he received his Eagle and we had Martin come back to his Eagle Court of Honor. Since then Trued's gone on to earn 51 merit badges and the Varsity Denali award, among many other awards. I attribute his determination to that first picture. Thank you!!! Our best wishes, Jerald, Lesa & Family"

"I am so sorry to hear of Bud's passing. I know that he could have not been in better care than with you all these years and that he, in turn, was a blessing to you and all those who were fortunate to meet him and share in his beauty. The heavens indeed have a new angel, may he soar with our hearts in tow. I'll be in touch. Take good care, Bonnie"

A Collection of Pictures

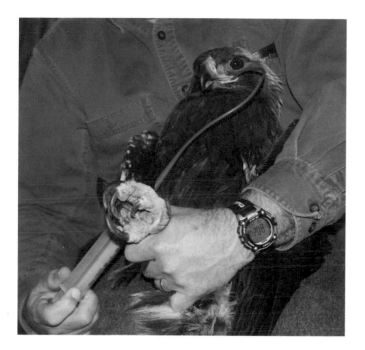

Critically ill golden eagle being tube fed by Martin Tyner (photos by Susan Tyner)

Golden eagle bites Martin's finger while being hand fed (photo by Susan Tyner)

Steve Dee receiving last minute instructions before eagle release (photos by Susan Tyner)

Rehabilitated golden eagle being released by Steve Dee (photos by Susan Tyner)

Martin Tyner removing golden eagle from rehabilitation facility (photo by Susan Tyner)

www.gowildlife.org

Preparing golden eagle for release (photo by Susan Tyner)

Glen Tyner preparing to release a large rehabilitated female golden eagle before his deployment to Iraq (photo by Susan Tyner)

In honor of our American Veterans, Steve Cantonwine, retired Marine Master Sergeant, prepares to release a young golden eagle who survived a shooting two months earlier (photo by Bonnie Bell)

Steve Cantonwine releases rehabilitated golden eagle back to the wild at Cedar Breaks National Monument (photo by Bonnie Bell)

135

Golden eagle, Scout, flying to the glove of Martin Tyner (4-photo sequence by Susan Tyner)

136

Martin exercising a young prairie falcon
(3-photo sequence by Noella Ballenger)

*Red tailed
hawk
illegally
caught
in coyote
trap
(photo by
Martin
Tyner)*

*Red tailed
hawk being
released
by Cassidy
Maxwell
(photos by
Martin Tyner)*

Sheri Shea releasing red tailed hawk (photos by Martin Tyner)

Sheri overcome with emotion after red tailed hawk release (photo by Martin Tyner)

Barn owl, hit by car, suffering from a concussion, being tube fed (photos by Susan Tyner)

After a few days the barn owl is feeling better and is being hand fed (photo by Susan Tyner)

Martin Tyner handing rehabilitated barn owl to Mark Browne (photo by Joanne Browne)

Mark Browne releasing rehabilitated barn owl (photos by Martin Tyner)

143

Martin Tyner tube feeding critically ill American white pelican (photo by Susan Tyner)

Pelican is feeling better (photo by Susan Tyner)

Removing pelican from airport kennel (photo by Susan Tyner)

Releasing pelican in Farmington Bay, Utah (photos by Susan Tyner)

Tube feeding turkey vulture (photo by Susan Tyner)

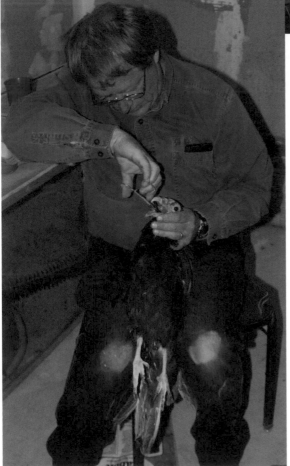

Hand feeding turkey vulture (photo by Susan Tyner)

Hand feeding turkey vulture (photo by Susan Tyner)

Turkey vulture in flight facility (photo by Martin Tyner)

One week old golden eaglet in the nest (photo by Martin Tyner)

Eleven week old golden eagle taking his first flight (photo by Martin Tyner)

Two baby Harris hawks from Martin's captive breeding program; left, one-hour old, right, one-week old (photo by Martin Tyner)

Three week old, orphaned prairie falcon that one day grows up to be a falcon named Horrible (photo by Steve Allred)

Orphaned kestrel falcons (photo by Martin Tyner)

Clutch of orphaned babies (photo by Susan Tyner)

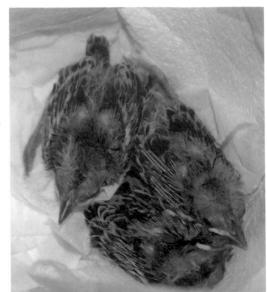

Baby with a voracious appetite (photo by Susan Tyner)

Orphaned baby barn owls at 3 weeks of age (photo by Martin Tyner)

Orphaned baby barn owls at 4 weeks of age (photo by Martin Tyner)

A clutch of orphaned barn owls, rescued and now ready for release (photo by Martin Tyner)

Orphaned baby flammulated owl, blown out of its nest by a thunder storm (photo by Martin Tyner)

Flammulated owl, now grown, released (photo by Martin Tyner)

Great horned owl injured in barbed wire fence (photo by Martin Tyner)

Rehabilitated, great horned owl released (photo by Martin Tyner)

Orphaned baby cottontail rabbits about five days old (photo by Susan Tyner)

Bottle raised orphaned mule deer (photo by Martin Tyner)

Feeding five week old, orphaned, baby cottontail rabbit, almost ready for release (photo by Susan Tyner)

Bottle raised,
orphaned coyote
(photos by Steve
Allred)

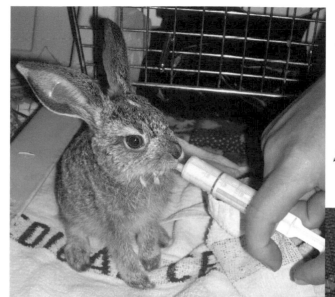

Feeding two week old, orphaned, baby jackrabbit (photo by Susan Tyner)

Feeding four week old, orphaned baby jackrabbit (photo by Stan Westfall)

Feeding orphaned, baby ground squirrel (photo by Martin Tyner)

Orphaned newborn prairie dog pup (photo by Martin Tyner)

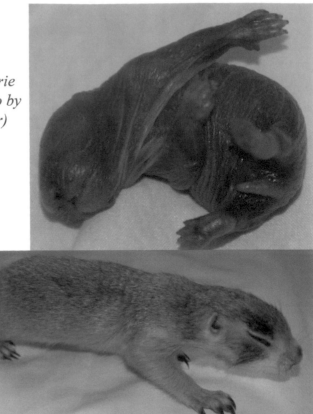

Orphaned prairie dog pup about twelve days of age (photo by Martin Tyner)

Orphaned prairie dog pup about two months of age (photo by Martin Tyner)

Peregrine falcon (photo by Martin Tyner)

Prairie falcon (photo by Martin Tyner)

Snowy egret (photo by Martin Tyner)

About the Authors

Vicki Swasey

At age twelve, Martin Tyner started caring for the sick, injured and orphaned creatures in his home town of Simi Valley, California. At age nineteen he was hired as curator of birds of prey at Busch Gardens, California. He worked in the movie and television industry training big cats, elephants, primates, sea mammals and raptors.

Martin is a federally licensed falconer, eagle falconer, wildlife rehabilitator, wildlife propagator, wildlife and environmental educator. He has been providing wildlife and environmental programs throughout the western United States, to schools, scouts and community groups for over forty years. He provides intergenerational Elderhostel programs through Dixie State College, has taught summer classes at Southern Utah University, "The Ancient Art of Falconry and Shakespeare", and performed in the Green Show with his raptors for the Utah Shakespearian Festival.

He is the founder of the Southwest Wildlife Foundation, which is a 501 c 3, non-profit, wildlife rescue, wildlife and environmental education organization. With the help of his golden eagle, Bud, they received a donation of 22.6 acres of beautiful canyon property from Utah Power/Scottish Power, for the development of a permanent wildlife rescue facility and a nature park for the children of Utah.

In 2005 Martin and Bud were honored by the Utah State Legislature for over a quarter-century of wildlife rescue and wildlife and environmental education in Utah.

In 1976 Martin met the love of his life, Susan, who is an animal lover in her own right. Susan Heaton Tyner began her career working with animals in 1977, as a bather-brusher at the Canine Castle, a local dog grooming shop, in Simi Valley and finished her training at the Pet Oasis, in Lancaster, California where she graduated to the position of professional dog groomer.

Susan and Martin moved to Cedar City, Utah in the winter of 1979 where they raised two children. In 1982, they opened Tyner's Pets and Dog Grooming where Martin ran the pet shop and Susan groomed dogs.

Susan volunteered as a leader in 4-H, developing the Guide Dog for the Blind puppy program in Southern Utah. She has been grooming dogs professionally for over thirty years and is an award winning international creative groomer.

If you would like to help the Southwest Wildlife Foundation as it cares for the sick, injured and orphaned creatures of Utah you may send a tax deductible donation to:

Southwest Wildlife Foundation
P.O. Box 1907
Cedar City, UT 84721-1907

Donations can also be made on line at www.gowildlife.org.

LaVergne, TN USA
15 December 2009
166874LV00001BB